INSTINCTIVE
QUILT ART

INSTINCTIVE QUILT ART

Using improvisational techniques to create vibrant art quilts

BETHAN ASH

BATSFORD

First published in the United Kingdom in 2011 by
Batsford, 10 Southcombe Street, London W14 0RA

An imprint of Anova Books Company Ltd

ISBN 978-1-84994-009-2

A CIP catalogue record for this book is available from
the British Library.

18 17 16 15 14 13 12 11
10 9 8 7 6 5 4 3 2 1

Reproduction by Dot Gradations Ltd, UK
Printed and bound by Craft Print International Ltd, Singapore

Greetings (detail) *(page 1)*
152 x 213cm (60 x 84in)
Inspired by the warmth of a Welsh welcome and made as a
tribute to the kindness and generosity shown by my family to
callers, guests and friends who came to visit; irrespective of
their race, creed or culture all were equally made welcome.

Down South (detail) *(page 2)*
122 x 91.5cm (48 x 36in)
See caption on page 95.

Orange Squares (detail) *(right)*
Detail of stitched collage using free-cut squares. The colours
used in the stitching are various shades of blues, crimsons and
rusts, which add depth, helping to separate the red, yellow and
lime foreground squares from the bright orange background.

CONTENTS

INTRODUCTION

Throw away the templates and use your imagination to create improvised art quilts and a whole new world is yours.

Don't let traditional concepts and ideals hold you back from real discoveries and new possibilities – take a step forward and choose a way of working in which everything can be done but nothing is 'wrong'. With today's focus on new technology, brilliant dyes and innovative fabrics, technique can tempt us – but by allowing your instincts and intuition to show you the way, you will come to realize that there is much more to quilt-making than piecing patterns or working to a repetitive grid. Give yourself the freedom to improvise; use your feelings for colour, shape and form and be spontaneous. Learn to appreciate the abstract method of fusing and use of colour and by doing so you will discover that your self-confidence grows as you become more accomplished. Become aware of quilt-making from another genre of thought – freely, spontaneously,

unconditionally and individually – and learn how to create collage in abstract designs using simple fusing techniques, which will result in free-form art quilts that are improvised, spontaneous and innovative.

To elevate a quilt or textile art above craft, we need to guide our work with critical decisions, empathy and every kind of intelligence. Enjoy the experience and challenge of working spontaneously, playing with ideas, colours, shapes and form, and appreciate that you are capable of free expression to create something unique completely by yourself. From the exercises in this book you can develop a new way of freely thinking and working that can totally change your outlook on quilt-making.

Please accept the challenge and discover what improvised quilt-making can mean for you. Enjoy yourself – it's easier than you think!

Bethan Ash

Hiraeth
(opposite and left [detail])
135 x 99cm (53 x 39in)
Inspired by my longing and nostalgia for all things Welsh, *Hiraeth* was designed and cut during quilting demonstrations I was giving in Japan. The technique I use of improvisational quilt-making was totally new to the watching Japanese audience. In this piece I've tried to convey the sheer enthusiasm and joy these people showed me, making me forget my homesickness for a while.

ABOUT THIS BOOK

Instinctive Quilt Art is designed to help you free your inner creativity so that you can fully engage in working with improvisation. Its underlying philosophy is that creative intuition is an instinct – a kind of inner compass or 'sixth sense' – that helps guide an artist's work. Everyone has his or her own natural intuition, which is a key asset in creating art. By letting go of preconceived ideas about quilt-making and tapping into your unique reserve of creative energy you can be free to explore new horizons in your work.

Abstract improvisation, by its expressiveness, fits perfectly into the current age. We are constantly looking for new forms of expression and attach value to freedom of action and innate or natural ingenuity. Nothing else offers the opportunity to satisfy this need like improvisation and abstract art.

This book covers abstraction, improvisation and collage techniques within contemporary art quilt-making, offering insights to anyone who wishes to broaden their understanding of the process of working spontaneously with colour, abstract forms and fused collage. I have kept the theoretical part short and included basic information relating to expressive and improvised elements of composition, colour, theme, and abstract form, which you will need to familiarize yourself with before completing the exercises. I then focus on abstraction and how it is used, in conjunction with collage and improvisational techniques, by exploring design concerns and themes common to artists, such as pattern, surface, form, composition, colour and texture.

Instinctive Quilt Art includes a series of simple hands-on exercises designed to help you develop your instincts for free-cut and fused collage. Rather than providing detailed step-by-step instructions that would inhibit your own creativity, each exercise consists of information on method, materials, composition, imagery and structure that will help you work in a directed way to the finished piece. The exercises are not trying to teach you how to cut a template, make a project using a particular technique, or copy a traditional design; instead they are intended to stimulate and nurture your instincts and intuition and allow these to become your trusted guides. You do not have to do the exercises in order, but rather should allow yourself the freedom to work on any that attract your curiosity. No restrictions of talent, skills, or prior art or stitching experience should stand in the way of choosing an exercise that has immediate appeal for you.

The ultimate goal of the exercises is to help you free yourself from the psychological barriers that inhibit creativity, and to open up a myriad of new and exciting possibilities for making quilt art. Use them as a starting point to understand the process and start making improvised collage, such as that illustrated in the small panels that make up the blocks used in the *Urban Landscape* deconstructed series, shown opposite.

Urban Landscape
99 x 122cm x 2.5cm
(39 x 48 x 1in)
This piece was inspired by the artist Hundertwasser's village design for Rolling Hills, Blumau, Styria. The work is first in a series connected to a recent house move from inner city living to the blissful calm of suburbia.

Most of the photographs in this book showcase a variety of artwork that I have created over the years. They illustrate the point that when you follow your intuition, you are more likely to create a picture that fits your own artistic personality rather than simply reproduce a picture from a book. Although most of the exercises tend to result in abstract images, all the exercises can be applied to any style of art practice. The connection with abstract art derives from the need to tap into the subjective aspect of one's intuition and to develop something visual out of pure imagination. The goal is not necessarily to make studies in abstract art, but rather to use freer and less restricted methods to enhance creative spontaneity and to increase the pleasure you experience during the process of making art.

Mandala series – Spring, Summer, Autumn, Winter
Each panel measures 50 x 50cm (19¾ x 19¾in)
This series forms a small part of a larger body of work that embraces printmaking, painting and collage as both a manifestation of our contemporary culture and a reflection of our past. The Mandala symbol evokes familiar memories, imparting context and values outside that of precious materials. Like touching heirlooms or viewing old photos, observance and tradition echo meaning within the symbol.

Featured throughout the book you will also find the work of other contemporary fibre artists from around the world, along with their comments on their own use of instinct when working. These works do not represent any particular style of instinctive or intuitive quilt-making – in fact they exemplify the diversity that can be achieved by using your intuition in creating artworks.

I hope this book will help you understand the abstract method of working and will also make you aware of other quilt-making genres. And that the exercises will motivate you to try improvisation and free expression and to begin to appreciate the value of your own instincts. The challenge is clear: you don't reap the rewards unless you actually do the work – so don't think about it, let's get started!

1 BEFORE WE BEGIN

WORKING SPONTANEOUSLY

I have been working with improvisation and fusing fabrics since the early 1990s. I like to work spontaneously, generally working without a predetermined design or pattern. This allows a piece of artwork to grow from my 'gut' rather than from a definitive sketch. Many of my art quilts have a more cerebral basis that depends heavily on the concept and the surface treatment I use. When making each new work I always search for a sense of movement, harmony and balance that encompasses a wide range of different approaches, from computer-manipulated imagery or using collage, to painting, printing and dyeing.

No matter what the basis of the art piece may be, I am continuously working to keep the process simple, fresh and stimulating by reinventing myself and the methods I use in quilt construction. A good way of practising improvised collage is to use scrap fabrics and offcuts from previous projects that have been pre-treated with fusible webbing, then simply building, layering and fusing multicoloured blocks. Multiples of these blocks can then be used as a starting point for a large quilt, or independently framed as a small collage, or made up as cushion fronts. I love working this way and would like to share it with you – you'll be surprised at how easy and addictive the method can be!

DISCLAIMER: Before I describe the 'tips and techniques' in this chapter it's important for me to emphasize that I'm not attempting to teach an art class in these pages. I'm giving you only the essential information you need to get started on a process; your curiosity, instinct and intuition can take it from there.

A place of your own

If possible, it's important to establish a place of your own where you can make your work, with few interruptions. There are really only a few things required for a home studio: privacy, adequate light (natural or artificial), a surface to work on, and enough room to step back and see what you're doing.

Even these requirements can be defined creatively: you can use the kitchen table, a part of the attic or cellar, or even a space set up in your garage. Over the years I have used every room in the house – fitting my space around the needs of my family – and I currently use a converted shed in our garden, which is the perfect set-up for me. If your space has to serve a dual function, like the kitchen or dining room, use drop cloths to protect surfaces, and keep your materials in portable containers for easy storage. Even though you may not have the ideal space for making artwork, you can create a space that is yours and that's the most important thing!

Taffiti Graffiti (detail)
91.5 x 122cm (36 x 48in)
Taffiti Graffiti is the first in a series of six works inspired by my love of graffiti as an art form and my interest in the decline and revival of the Welsh language. It is a little known fact that Welsh has been spoken for longer than any other language in Europe. In addition, the work is about how I see colour in relationship to shape, line and linear movements.

Garden shed/studio – my *Ty bach* (small house)

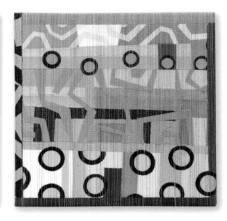

Why quilt-making?

It is meaningful to me that quilt-making is a woman's art and heritage and that we are but one link in a long chain and tradition of women expressing their opinions and feelings in cloth, needle and thread. Quilt-making is a good way for you to express yourself. It's an art form that allows you to work with fabric; quilts are tactile, they have plenty of colour and texture – they have all those things that other mediums don't have.

TECHNIQUES AND TIPS FOR WORKING WITH FABRIC

Fusing fabric

Fusing fabric is a direct medium and is a very easy technique to use. You can go directly from any image or any idea that you have in your head to making an artwork. In traditional quilt-making you generally piece or sew things together, but with fusing if you want to join two fabrics you just overlap them and press with an iron, so it's very quick and easy. The technique is similar to painting in that you layer colour upon colour upon colour, creating a multicolour feast of collage. You can work swiftly and, of course, as an artist the more work you make the better you get and the more confident you feel – and this is a great way to be.

Some brands of fusible webbing are difficult to stitch through or change the surface of your fabric. I use Appliqué It, but also recommend Bondaweb (Wonder Under); for lightweight silks I use Misty Fuse and a Teflon pressing sheet. Choose 100% cotton fabrics with no finish; hand-dyed and batik fabrics work best because the colour penetrates through the fabric. Fabrics with a higher thread count also fuse better and fray less when cut.

• Wash and iron your fabric to remove any starch before fusing – do not use fabric softener.
• Fuse your fabrics by ironing the rough side of the webbing to the reverse side of the fabric, using a dry hot iron (cotton

Sticks 'n' Stones
Each panel measures 30 x 30 x 2.5cm (12 x 12 x 1in)
This collage is based on horizontal and vertical lines and combines curves and circles within the design.

setting). Evenly press from the centre to the outer edges and iron for seven seconds – if unsure, follow the instructions that come with the webbing.

• Too much heat applied repeatedly will weaken the glue, burn it into the fabric, change the fabric colour or make the fabric stiff. Also, over-fused fabric will no longer adhere to other fabrics.

• To protect your ironing board and iron, place a sheet of greaseproof paper under and on top of the fabric when fusing.

• Fabric that bubbles or ripples when fused will flatten out when the release (backing) paper is peeled off.

• Always let the fabric and webbing cool before you come to remove the release (backing) paper.

• Remove the release (backing) paper in one piece by first fanning with a finger and then swiping your hand between the fabric and paper. Feel for any gummy areas that the iron didn't cover and re-fuse these.

• If the webbing separates from the release (backing) paper, it is still usable. Just place the webbing on the fabric, put the release (backing) paper on top and fuse into place.

• Save the release (backing) paper – it can be fused to over and over again. Use it for assembling fused collages, storing fused scraps, protecting the ironing board and pattern-making. You can fuse to either side of Wonder Under release (backing) paper.

• If you leave the paper on when cutting out a pattern piece, remove it easily by gently slicing the paper in the centre of the fabric with the tip of your scissors and peeling from the centre.

• Always use sharp scissors and rotary cutter blades – blunt tools fray the fabric.

• Cut webbing-backed fabrics webbing side up when using a rotary cutter, so the glue side does not stick to the mat and cause the fabric to fray when it is removed. It is also easier to see the areas where there is no glue.

• When cutting a pile of webbing-backed fabric, do not stack with the webbing sides together or the pieces may be difficult to separate. Up to three layers of backed fabric shapes can be cut out at one time.

• Dark fabrics may cast a shadow if placed under light fabrics, so whenever possible overlap dark over light.

• Fuse-tack elements for only five seconds and with little pressure.

• Elements that are fuse-tacked can be easily removed, although some fibres and glue may remain on the base fabric.

• Save all your fused scraps. They are great for tiny elements and collage work.

WARNING!

• It is vitally important to keep your iron and ironing surface clean and free of fusible webbing otherwise the glue may transfer to the surface of your quilt.

• Keep your iron clean with Iron Off or any other suitable cleaner that is good for removing glue.

Lines and Cubes
Each panel measures 30 x 30 x 2.5cm (12 x 12 x 1in)
These blocks have evolved from splatter-painted fabric and free-cut squares.

Ltd Edition
99 x 99cm (39 x 39in)
A one-of-a-kind collage,
inspired by a piece of
printed fabric by Dutch
textile artist Els Van Baarle.

Collage

Collage is so well known and popular that it needs practically no introduction; I am not going to elaborate on any exotic collage techniques or write at length about the philosophy of the art of collage. It is quite accessible and easy to work with, and you don't have to know many sophisticated techniques in order to use collage in your work. Its beauty is that it appeals to all people – anyone from the hobbyist to the fine artist can use collage techniques to add creativity and dimension to their work. Just work spontaneously and give yourself the freedom to change your mind as the collage progresses, just as you might if you were doing a painting. This medium can be a lot of fun, as long as you don't feel obliged to follow the rules.

• Start with a single piece of either plain or patterned fabric that inspires you and build your collage around it.
• Source your fabrics and choose colours that please you, even if they don't make literal sense. Play with other colours against those you've chosen – there is no law that says you need colour to be literally correct, even in a realistic landscape.
• Pay attention to colour value (the lightness or darkness of a colour). Strong, well-placed value contrasts can give your work more zing than using similar values.
• Pre-back your fabrics with fusible webbing before you begin cutting.
• Cut your source material into various shapes with scissors or a rotary cutter. Cut along the contours of forms in printed fabric or cut out abstract shapes. A greater variance of shapes and sizes will enhance the visual impact of your collage.
• Use a good, firm foundation before you start applying the details. I use a medium-weight interfacing, but you can use different weights, depending on the finish you want to achieve. Lightweight interfacing is soft and drapes well, making it suitable for lap quilts, bedspreads or clothing. Heavyweight (pelmet) interfacing is much firmer and will hang flat with no drooping, so it is better for wall art.
• If you need to do a drawing first, even a detailed one, do it. But try not to let a

Dear Sir
61 x 122cm (24 x 48in)
The work in this series zooms in on the flow of a shorthand scribble, cropping a specific gesture and focusing its energy in a terse statement. At times the line is strongly directional and sharp, at others the forms curve and turn around each other.

drawing paralyse you – if you feel like departing from it halfway through your collage, by all means do so. A collage can take on a life of its own, so no matter what your original idea was, try to be open-minded.

• If you fuse down a detail and it doesn't seem to work well, go with your instincts; re-work and do what you feel is right for the composition.

• If you're dealing with mostly rectangular shapes, try using a few diagonals or curves for contrast and relief.

• Evaluate your collage for cohesiveness and overall design. Add more collage elements if it needs more colours or layers.

• Don't hesitate to cover up your mistakes with overlay. The beauty of collage is that you can put on all the layers you need to get a result you're happy with.

• Stitch, paint or print on your collage to create a multimedia effect. Use acrylic paints rather than Procion MX dyes for the best results.

• Enhance your collage further by adding embellishments. These can range from shop-bought items to found objects at a jumble sale – or use natural elements, including shells or dried flowers. Set your imagination free when making your collage.

• Save your leftover pre-treated fabric wastage and off-cuts for future projects.

• Try mounting and framing small works to give them a presence.

SURFACE DESIGN

Surface design techniques can be used to create unique original fabrics for your art quilts. Common ways of embellishing the fabric surface include dyeing, painting and printing, and there are also newer methods such as digital image transfer and laser technology. Some techniques have many different approaches and the information here not only gives a brief explanation of each but will also give you inspiration and ideas on how each technique can be used.

Digital transfer

Iron-on transfers originated in the T-shirt industry as a means of personalizing clothing, but it is now possible to create your own transfers at home using your computer, scanner and printer. Drawings, photographs, actual objects and computer-generated imagery can all be printed using heat-sensitive transfer paper – anything you can lay flat on the glass of the scanner can be turned into a transfer, including objects such as feathers, leaves, flowers, fibres, cloth; the possibilities are endless. Art books and magazines are a source of both inspiration and material that can be used in your work.

Shopaholic (see below) started off as a simple layered paper collage, using magazine images of designer items. The collage was then scanned, printed and heat-transferred onto plain cloth and finally stitched and quilted. The work was inspired by my best friend's compulsion to shop – especially for designer items!

• The process is simple – first choose pictures from the sources around you; magazine or colour photographs work well for original artwork.
• Put together pages or make a collage of images. If you keep pictures of similar things together – such as a sheet of birds, a sheet of fibres – you will have a library you can use again and again. Store scanned images in file folders on your computer, labelled by subject.
• Cut out pictures of things you might incorporate into a design, and glue the pictures onto an A4 (letter-size) piece of paper using a glue stick. Leave a wide margin around the edges of each image and trim off any unwanted background.
• Scan the page and print it out onto A4 (letter) photo transfer paper, following the manufacturer's printing instructions.

Shopaholic – Shop 'til you Drop!
20 x 173cm (8 x 68in)
Inspired by and dedicated to my friend Alison, who is a very stylish lady and loves to shop — especially for shoes, make-up, clothing and all kinds of designer items. We met and studied fashion together at art college in the 1960s and have been great friends ever since — just wish I had her taste and style!

- Set your printer settings at the highest quality, and set the printer properties to print a mirror image. Once you have printed the transfers, carefully cut out the individual images.
- Press your background fabric to remove any wrinkles, then iron the transfer images face down onto the fabric following the manufacturer's instructions.
- Allow the images to cool and peel off the paper coating – your finished design is now ready for stitching and finishing.
- On heavyweight and more textured fabrics it may not be necessary to trim pictures so completely – the rougher texture of the cloth will obscure the edge of the motif.
- Iron-on transfers work well on smooth, evenly woven natural or synthetic fabrics. Using light-coloured fabrics will produce better results.
- To make large-scale prints, copy your project onto a CD or memory stick and have it commercially printed. In some cases, you may be able to email the project directly to a commercial printer.

Right: Three examples of paper collage, using cut and layered images from magazines.

Action painting

Spontaneous creativity for pure pleasure, action painting is just what the name suggests: painting with complete abandon, dripping and spilling colours all over the surface with no particular idea or plan in mind. It is nothing more than letting the paint do what it wants to do with a little help from you. Action painting emphasizes the dynamics of the painting process with a focus on movement, gesture, and expressive free play. This approach is a good place to start using your intuition because it allows you to use materials freely and to explore movement, spontaneity and dynamic change without exerting overt control over the painting process. Because you want to maximize your use of intuition in these exercises, you need to set aside any vestiges of technical control and critical judgment that might get in the way of making this experience as spontaneous, free-flowing and energetic as possible. Like many of the exercises in this book, you don't really need step-by-step instructions to engage in this intuitive process – just begin and see where it goes.

Can You Hear the Birds Sing?
**99 x 99cm x 2.5cm
(39 x 39 x 1in)**
Detail of a quilt made in protest against the effect global warming is having on our bird population and wildlife. The circular spheres and strong colour combinations of reds and oranges convey a sense of the heat of the sun, against the blue of the sky.

• Before starting, make sure you have a large area available, and put down a drop cloth or newspapers to protect the floor or table surface.

• Use inexpensive fabrics like curtain lining or butcher paper (newsprint) to catch your action painting so that you do not worry too much about wasting paint or materials that you may or may not want to use.

• Begin with the easiest form of action painting, by simply soaking a brush with paint and dripping and splashing paint onto your cloth. Let the paint splatter and drip as you make bold, impromptu gestures, or change to more subtle patterns of movement to see what kinds of marks the gestures create.

• Try using brushes of different sizes and paints of different colours, and let your marks merge together on the cloth.

• The first few times you try action painting should be purely experimental, and don't expect that a predictable picture will take form from this process. The important thing to remember is that unpredictability is what you are after, so you can revel in the pure enjoyment of playing with the paint.

• Begin to experiment with different approaches: try flinging paint off the brush to create explosive splatters, dripping paint from different heights, or pouring paint of different thicknesses (diluted with various amounts of water) onto the cloth at the same time.

Abstract Tie (detail)
122 x 183cm (48 x 72in)
The palette in this piece is a complementary one and even though the work is pieced there are still elements of rhythm.

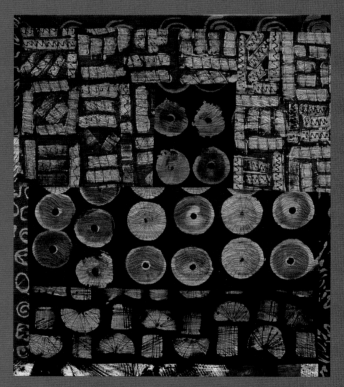

Removed 1/08 *(top)*
Cynthia Corbin
81 x 61cm (32 x 24in)
This piece was inspired by the luscious colour of a piece of rich gold fabric that the artist found in her stash, with a hunk cut out of it.

Paint Job *(above)*
Cynthia Corbin
51 x 53cm (20 x 21in)
While experimenting with paint sticks, Cynthia painted every inch of this piece after the quilting was done. While the work was crazy and chaotic, she found the seam lines caught her interest, so that's where she put the buttons.

Blocked *(top)*
Cynthia Corbin
61 x 61cm (24 x 24in)
Again this was inspired by the fabric. *Blocked* was developed through intensive machine quilting, which has given it a 'shed door' pattern.

Black Top *(above)*
Cynthia Corbin
89 x 76cm (35 x 30in)
Cynthia likes to play with the relationship of the form to the field surrounding it. In *Black Top*, it is the scale of pattern in the discharged fabrics that defines the form against the field.

Print techniques

The art of printmaking is widely practised by artists at all levels because of its unique visual properties, as well as the element of surprise that comes with it. The techniques described here use direct hand-printing methods and do not need a press or other expensive equipment. The prints made can remain as one-offs or be embellished with Markal Paintstiks, additional colours or stitching techniques to create the finished work. As with other techniques presented in this book, the emphasis is on using your intuition and spontaneity to spark your artistic creativity. For examples of what can be achieved with print, see the mixed-media artworks of American quilt artist Cynthia Corben on the opposite page. Cynthia says of her work, 'I love going to my pile of bits and pieces, not editing too much – just to see what is there.'

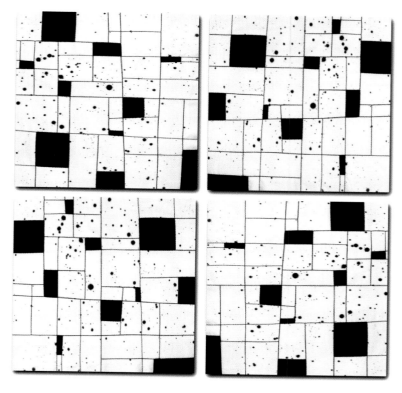

White Square Splatter
Each block measures 30 x 30cm (12 x 12in)
Example of blocks evolving from splatter-painted fabric and free-cut shapes.

Inkblot printing

Probably the easiest and most accessible print process is that of inkblot transfers, or so-called Rorschach prints. These types of prints are made by dripping, splattering or brushing ink randomly onto one half of your cloth and then folding it in half while the medium is still wet to make the print – nothing could be easier.

• When you put your medium (ink or paint) on the cloth, experiment with making shapes of different sizes, colours and with varying amounts of medium.
• Also try using different tools and techniques to apply your medium – rags, sponges, an ink roller, a painting knife, scraps of cardboard, etc.
• You can layer different blots by folding and refolding the cloth several times to build up the depth of the image.
• Starting with these suggestions, you can invent your own techniques, which can be developed into varied and beautiful compositions.

Monoprinting

This process takes the method of direct-transfer printmaking used in the previous exercise one step further. The difference is that you apply ink or paint to a separate surface and transfer it to another surface to make your print.

• First try using a heavy piece of paper or cardboard as your printing plate. Paint it with thick, gooey brushstrokes and then press it onto your cloth or canvas.
• Get different effects either by changing the type and viscosity of the paint or ink that you use or by modifying the time you take before making the transfer.
• For a different variation on this technique, use slick surfaces such as glass, Plexiglas, aluminium foil, wax paper, or sheet metal as your plate. Surfaces like these release the paint medium more completely than more absorbent materials. Experiment by using various materials as your printing plate, to discover your own preferences.

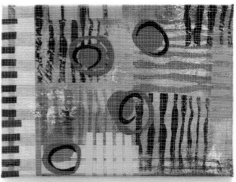

Interweave – 1, 2, 3 + 4
Series of four blocks, each measuring 30 x 40 x 2.5cm (12 x 16 x 1in)
The shapes applied to the silk-screened fabric are based on horizontal and vertical lines interpreting movement and the juxtaposition of simple forms.

Screen printing

Screen printing is a printing technique that uses a fine woven mesh stretched on a frame, which supports an ink-blocking stencil. The design of the stencil includes impermeable and open areas, so ink or other printable materials can be pressed through the open areas of mesh using a roller or squeegee to create a sharp-edged image on a substrate beneath. Screen printing is also known as silkscreen and serigraph printing.

Resist techniques

With resist techniques, shapes or designs are created directly on the fabric using a resist medium that is impermeable to the ink or other printing medium that is being used to add colour to the work. Some resist techniques are completely random, others will allow varying degrees of control over the final result.

Salt resist

This is a wet-on-wet flow-repelling and suction technique – if salt is scattered on wet paint it absorbs the paint, which results in a lighter ring of colour forming around the salt grain. This produces an interesting texture effect within the flow of colour. For an example of work using painted Habotai, silk and salt resist, see the *Windows* quilt opposite.

• For best results stretch the cloth over a wooden painting frame before you begin.
• Start applying strokes of colour with a wide brush. Work quickly and completely to cover the cloth with wet ink; when painting, use variation and contrast.
• Next, randomly scatter sea salt onto the wet surface. Twist and tip the frame so that the colours run in new directions.
• Lightly spray over the entire area with water and then scatter more salt into the wet paint. Allow the work to dry.
• Finally wipe off the dried salt grains, removing as much of the salt as possible or it will continue to attract fluid and bubbles – or may even cause mould to form on your work.

Windows
76 x 99cm (30 x 39in)
Inspired by the patterns
left on window panes after
a shower of rain. Here you
can see that when using
salt resist with simple
shapes and colours, the
result can be completely
abstract.

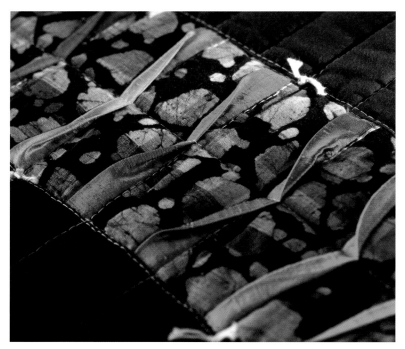

Wax candle resist

Another simple resist technique, this is based on using wax to prevent the dye, paint or ink penetrating to certain areas of the fabric.

• Design a composition using clear, simple shapes and draw it onto plain cotton using a thin pencil line. Trace over the lines with a wax candle, pressing down well so that a wax layer remains on the cloth. The wax will repel wet paint or dye so it will remain outside the lines.
• Another variation is to warm the candle, then shake and flick melted wax over the surface.
• For best results stretch the cloth over a wooden painting frame before you start painting.
• Cover the design with paint, ink or dye (you can even use all three) using random strokes and splodges.
• You can also scatter salt over the wet surface, as described in the salt resist technique on page 24. When the ink is dry, wipe off the salt grains to remove them entirely.
• Cover the design with newspaper and press with a hot iron to remove the wax. Repeat this process until all the wax is completely removed.

Rust dyeing

This is another surface colouring method that can be used to add dimension to your fabrics and fibres. You can place any rusty object next to wet fabric and acquire rust patterning over time – the process can create ten or more natural colours, depending on what was adjacent to the iron ore. Natural fibres take rust colours better than synthetic fibres and you can rust dye onto commercially dyed and/or printed fabrics as long as they do not have an anti-stain coating. For an example of how wonderfully stunning this process can look, see the work by Danish quilt artist Charlotte Yde shown opposite.

• Wear gloves and a mask when working with rust – you can become gravely ill from too much contact with raw iron products. In addition, tolerance to raw iron varies with each person.
• When applying rusty objects to naturally dyed fabrics the colours will change. Iron – rust – is a modifier and is used as a mordant (colour fixer) with natural dyes.
• Rust dyeing with water takes about a week. Using vinegar will produce colour in less time – usually 24 hours – because it aids in breaking the rust particles free from the object that is rusting.

Kimono – sampler
198 x 173cm (79 x 68in)
Details of sampler showing examples of resist, batik and tie-dyed fabrics.

• Use undiluted white vinegar and all sorts of rusty objects to acquire rust-dyed patterns. Old nails and wire work well for this technique.

• Wire can be used for bound resist techniques, especially when wrapping the fabric around a rusty pipe.

• If you want to push the rust-dyeing technique further, rinse the fabric and neutralize it in salt water, rinse it again and then rust the fabric once more. Working in stages will help prevent the fabric from rotting through.

• If you want the rust dyeing process to stop you need to neutralize it with a salt-water solution. Dissolve about ¼ cup salt into four gallons of hot water in a five-gallon bucket. Rinse your fabric and then soak in the salt water for about 15 minutes.

• Finally, wash the fabric using a non-phosphorous soap or a mild colour-free shampoo. Let the fabric dry for 24 hours.

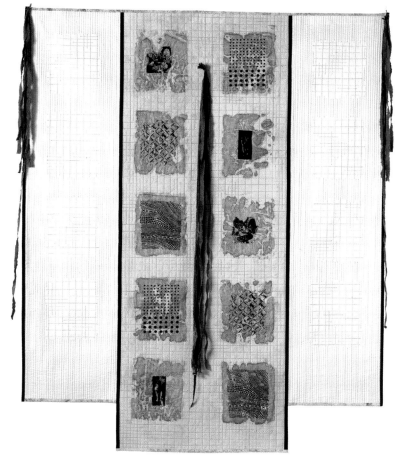

Imprints of Time 1 + 2
Charlotte Yde (Denmark)
Two pieces, each 172 x 140cm (67¾ x 55in)
In her rust series Charlotte has been interested in the time aspect and the unpredictability of the process. Unlike most other textile artists, who are using rust as a colouring agent, she has been constantly trying to create patterns and not just using the colour.

GIVING A PROFESSIONAL FINISH

Blocking a quilt

Art quilts, with all their surface design and heavy quilting, sometimes need blocking to create a flatter surface. The quilt can be blocked and then squared up, or it can be squared up and then blocked. Depending on the size of the quilt, blocking can be done on a design wall or on a carpeted floor. The secret is to let the quilt dry out completely on the flat surface.

- Evenly pin the quilt to the surface, placing pins every 5–10cm (2–4in).
- Using a spray bottle, spray the surface lightly with water, then allow the quilt to dry completely.
- If the quilt is completely flat, then it is finished.
- If not, you may need to use a steam iron or steamer over the pinned surface and then again allow it to dry completely.

Sleeve construction

When hanging a wall quilt you will need a 16cm (6¼in) wide sleeve running along the top edge of the quilt on the reverse – this enables an acrylic batten to be inserted through the sleeve and then screwed to the wall. On larger wall quilts, you may also want to add a narrow sleeve at the bottom to take an acrylic rod to help the quilt hang straight on the wall.

Yellow Circle (detail)
122 x 81cm (48 x 32in)
An art quilt inspired by over-dyed fabrics.

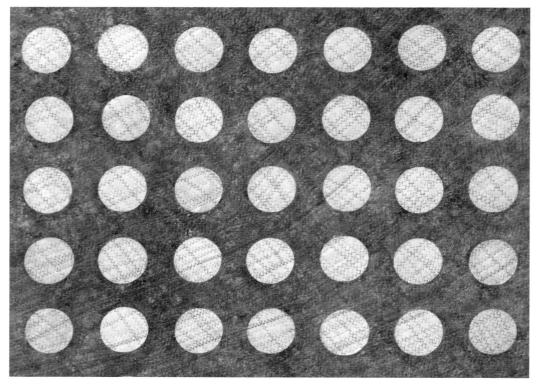

Everyday is Sunday (detail)
99 x 99 x 2.5cm (39 x 39 x 1in)
Another piece made in protest against global warming, but here the cooler, more harmonious colours suggest a calm, repetitive feeling. The small dots in the painting flow freely across the canvas, resembling the look of a field from the air. The field has been intruded upon by the famous crop circle phenomenon, which is shown by the slender white circles that are layered onto the surface.

Framing small works

Small works usually look better if they are framed.

• Choose a wooden stretcher frame that is about 12.5cm (5in) smaller overall than the finished piece of work.
• Lay the work face side down and place the stretcher frame on top in the centre. Fold the collage over the frame at one of the sides and staple it in the centre of the frame.

• Use pliers to pull the canvas taut and staple in the centre on the opposite side. Do the same for the remaining sides, pulling the canvas taut each time.
• Staple along each side, working from centre to end each time and placing the staples about 2.5cm (1in) apart.
• Fold the collage over neatly at the corners and place a staple over the fold.
• To neaten the raw edges, cover with cotton tape and stick down.

Colour Block
Each block measures 30 x 30 x 2.5cm (12 x 12 x 1in)
Detail of four blocks in a series of 16 – see the full series on page 42. Making simple preparatory blocks is always a good way to explore the potential of a design and to test out different materials.

EXERCISE 1: USING SIMPLE SHAPES

A good way of practising improvised collage is to use scrap fabrics and off-cuts from previous projects that have been pre-treated with fusible webbing. Simply build up the design by layering and fusing at random to create multicoloured blocks. Multiples of these blocks can then be used as a starting point for a large quilt, independently framed as a small collage, or made up into cushion fronts. A simple yet very effective pattern can be built up by using irregularly shaped square and rectangular pieces of plain fabric. These instructions are for a basic 45 × 45cm (18 × 18in) block similar to those shown in the cushion collection images opposite.

Materials and equipment

- 45 × 45cm (18 × 18in) each of plain cotton, iron-on medium-weight interfacing, wadding (batting) or interlining, and calico (muslin) for the backing
- A selection of pre-fused plain colour cotton fabrics
- Sharp scissors or a rotary cutter, mat and acrylic ruler (whichever you prefer working with)
- Iron and ironing board
- Greaseproof (bakery) paper to protect your iron and board when fusing fabrics
- Pressing cloth and spray gun
- Sewing machine
- Assorted machine embroidery threads (floss)

Method

1. Prepare your foundation background by ironing the rough side of the interfacing to the wrong side of the plain fabric square.
2. Select a quantity of pre-fused cotton fabrics. Take your scissors or rotary cutter and free cut these into assorted squares of different sizes. Repeat until you have more than enough squares to cover the background. Sort the squares into piles of the same size and store in plastic envelopes – you can keep any leftovers for future projects.
3. Place your background square, right side up, on an ironing board or working surface. Peel the backing papers off some of the squares and start to cover the background, placing the pieces right side up and rough side down. Layer in a sequence of the largest down first, overlap with the medium and finish with the smallest.
4. Use your eye to place and layer the colours, working from the centre to the outer edges. Periodically cover the design with greaseproof (bakery) paper and hot press to anchor the shapes as you layer.
5. Use your imagination when placing the squares: scatter, overlap, or leave spaces to allow the background to show through.
6. Once you are satisfied with the placement, cover with a cloth, spray and press with a hot iron so that the design is firmly anchored into position.
7. To prepare for stitching, place the calico (muslin) backing right side down, add the layer of wadding (batting) or interlining, then place the collage on top, right side up. Pin the layers together.
8. Stitch randomly through the layers a multitude of times, using straight stitch and a variety of coloured threads (floss) and taking the pins out as you go. Repeat this process until the background is stitched to your satisfaction, making sure you have covered any raw edges in the design.
9. Finally, press again and trim any thread ends. The block is now ready to be turned into a cushion, a small hanging or used as part of a larger-scale quilt.

Cushion Collection
Assorted silk cushions
made using squares of
plain coloured fabric.

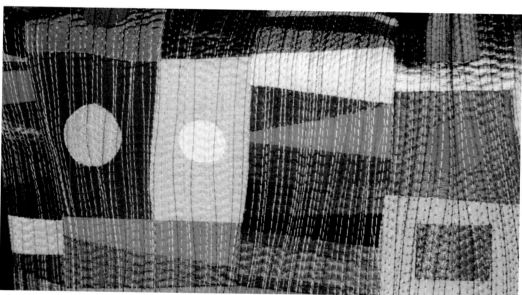

2 INSTINCTIVE ABSTRACTS

AN IMPROVISED APPROACH

We are used to traditional quilts having a meaning and containing images that we can readily react to and form an opinion about. But with abstract art, in which the shapes and forms are invented to a greater or lesser degree, the process of viewing and responding can seem more complicated. It is understandable that, given the long tradition of traditional quilt-making and the fact that most quilts have a narrative content, some people find it extremely difficult to adopt the freer approach that instinctive, abstract quilt-making demands. Also, we sometimes search for meaning where in fact there is none: many abstract artworks focus purely on the visual and emotional delights of colour and related formal elements.

Applying the lbs (Cutting The Carbs series) (right)
145 x 145cm (57 x 57in)
This is the third quilt in a series of work based around self-identity. All my life I have battled with my weight/size problem. I have followed every diet under the sun – sometimes successfully, other times not. This series of work has been created in homage to brave dieters everywhere!

A Minute on the Lips (Cutting The Carbs series) (left)
Each piece 38 x 15 x 15cm (15 x 6 x 6in)
A 3D installation of capsule-shape bolsters, part of a series of work based on obesity and self-identity.

ABSTRACTS TOUCHING FIGURATIVE

To follow the abstract method of improvisation does not mean that you only have to work in an abstract way; on the contrary, the method and exercises in this book are designed to help you develop your artistic skills and feelings for colour, shape, texture, composition and harmony. The more you practise these skills the better your work will be, even if you work figuratively. Abstract improvisation also stimulates the experimental and expressive approach to figurative reality and leads to the creation of something wholly individual and unique.

The range of the improvised approach is so broad that figurative and total abstraction can exist side by side without any problems. It is simply a matter of personal preference. I use both approaches in my work, a freedom I have allowed myself in order to keep alive each form of expression. For me, new art has to be original. I believe the work says something about the artist. As the works in this book show, my interests lie in interpreting different subjects through the power of colour combined with effective and, hopefully, exciting composition.

The pieces by Canadian artist Jayne Willoughby Scott shown left demonstrate her wonderful sense of humour and colour sense. She says of her work: 'I see each of my pieces of art as a "meditation". Each represents a study of something – rumination about the materials, ideas for future projects, and ruminations about personal or social issues of concern to me at that time. It is the solitude and the repetition of making stitches and marks on paper, canvas, fabric or whatever materials I am working with which allows for the quiet sifting of thoughts and free flow of ideas.'

Death by Chocolate
Jayne Willoughby Scott
91.5 x 61cm (36 x 24in)
The Pacific Northwest Quilt Association had a fundraiser where the raffle quilts had a theme of 'earth, wind, fire and chocolate'. This was the result of Jayne's experimentation with machine appliqué, quilting and embroidery as embellishment.

Lunch on the Run
Jayne Willoughby Scott
59.5 x 59cm (23½ x 23in)
Since she loves to cook and to eat good food – and also to create art with fabric – Jayne tried to bring these creative passions together with *Lunch on the Run*.

IMPROVISATION AND ABSTRACT ART IN CONTEXT

There are abstract qualities in many forms of artwork. If you examine almost any work of art you will find passages within it that are essentially abstract – perhaps patches of colour, form, stitch or brushwork – which are intended to suggest something but only succeed in implying this because of the content and detail in the wider context of the work. The abstract procedure allows a fairly direct approach to the essential conditions for creating improvised art quilts, since total abstraction is completely reliant on information from our inner being and is therefore in direct contact with creativity, expressiveness, originality and individuality. When you work figuratively, your actions are guided by external information – you can see the details of the design, the dimensions, shape and colour in front of you. This information determines your actions. Your feeling for shape and colour is barely consulted, because the desired effect is already visually available. You use only your technical skill to produce on the flat surface what you observe externally.

Cell U Lite
173 x 91.5cm (68 x 36in)
Part of a series of work created in homage to brave dieters everywhere – here again the subject of dieting has been used for inspiration. In order to achieve the degree of colour intensity required, I paint my fabrics with acrylic and also use Procion MX dyes on silk.

As soon as you start to work completely in abstract there is no external information available at all. You will have to devise shape, colour, texture and composition yourself and for this you must consult your inner resources and therefore work from within yourself. This is the principle behind abstract improvisation. The improvised method encourages free and expressive quilt-making; even if you do not have a great deal of technical experience, or have not completed an art course, using the improvised method will develop your feeling for colour, shape, expression, movement and so on. To fully explore these elements in your own work will perhaps require a different way of looking and thinking, and this can be encouraged to develop by viewing a wide range of work by some of today's contemporary abstract artists.

The total freedom of action within this school adds an extra dimension to your quilting experience. As you are not bound to traditional methods, your creativity is given far more scope. A main feature of this method, therefore, is studying and consciously learning to deal with the abstract elements that together determine your work. Because there are no restraints, abstract offers the ideal basis for experimenting, building up technical know-how and experience.

Such experiments also cultivate your own sources of inspiration and are designed to help you free your creativity so that you can fully engage in making art. The work on the following pages is by Swiss quilt artist and teacher Maryline Collioud-Robert; her expert use of colour, shape and movement define, energize and animate the surface of her quilts.

Stamps 2
Maryline Collioud-Robert
83 x 105.5cm
(32½ x 41½ in)
In this series the thread (floss) used to embroider the small pieces is important, as it plays a part in the colour contrasts. The blanket stitch emphasizes the textile quality of the piece.

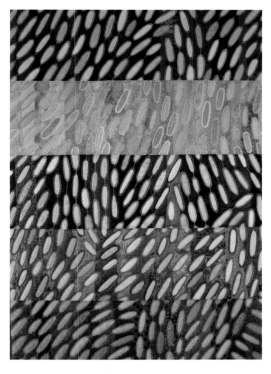

Collage 3
Maryline Collioud-Robert
124 x 84cm (49 x 33in)
In this quilt Maryline started by choosing the five groups of colours and then played with the shapes, since she likes to combine colour and movement.

Ciao Bella!
Maryline Collioud-Robert
Three panels, each 109 x 35cm (43 x 13¾in)
Maryline likes to work with vivid colours and she is interested in the contrasts that happen between colours when they are put on top of one another.

MODERN METHODS

Looking back over the development of Western art, the first real signs of abstraction can be detected in the work of the Impressionists. Their whole approach to their work, both technically and philosophically, marked a complete break with the academic traditions of the time, particularly in their use of colour and their interest in colour theories. The principal interest of the Impressionists was in the effect of light on the surface of objects and how this momentary quality could be captured through an analysis of tone and colour. One of their most significant technical innovations was to abandon traditional ideas of composition and drawing. In creating a sense of shimmering light and colour, they had to dispense with the accepted practice of delineating objects, because any firm outlines would divide the surface too positively and detract from the atmospheric quality they sought.

There is great value in studying the development of 20th-century abstract art. Abstraction in itself is an interesting subject, which reveals ideas and techniques that can contribute to your own work. There are many books on the subject and most major galleries have abstract paintings in their collections. Galleries such as Tate Modern, London, and the Museum of Modern Art, New York, actually specialize in abstract and other forms of modern art.

Rhosyn Du –
Black Rose
152 x 213cm (60 x 84in)
Made in memoriam to the Bridgend youngsters: the colours, black, white and violet represent despair, youth and mourning. Just as shapes can be simple, so can the colour. It is often more effective to restrict the colour range to just a few colours.

Chasing the Dragon
101.5 x 90cm (40 x 35in)
This quilt symbolizes addiction and the feelings it evokes. Colour, shape and form are essential elements in any type of quiltmaking, and particularly in abstract work. Freedom of expression and a sense of movement are also paramount. Acquired by the Museum of Art and Design (MAD), New York.

When looking at abstract art many people do not realize the skill involved in the process, but after trying to achieve the same effect you will quickly come to understand and appreciate that there is much more to abstraction or improvisation than just putting colours and shapes together. Abstraction comes from knowledge and experience of art partnered with hard work and means something different to each artist or maker, but ultimately it comes from the same place – the heart.

Figurative work is more easily understood and also generally considered to be more skilful than abstract work. However, a different sort of skill is needed in the making of abstract work – the ability to be selective. Selection is fundamental when working with abstraction; whether or not the subject matter is recognizable, for instance a particular landscape or an expression of emotion or feeling, abstraction comes about as the artist selects what to leave in or out. Through this process, the work becomes simpler and simpler until what is left is the essence of the original source as perceived by the artist.

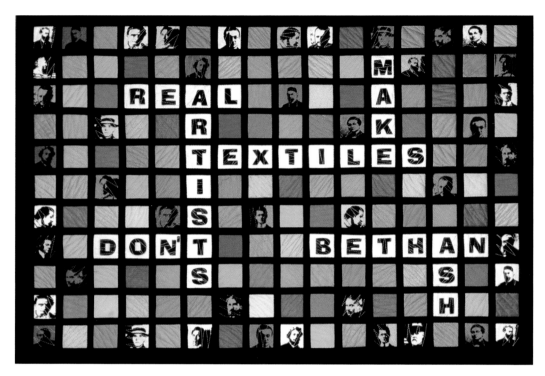

Real Artists Don't Make Textiles
63.5 x 91.5cm (25 x 36in)
Inspiration for this piece came from the title of a work by tapestry weaver Anne Jackson. At the time (the early 1990s) the phrase was frequently used by the British art establishment. The quilt features images of these famous painters: Bazille, Cézanne, Chagal, Degas, Duchamp, Janco, Johns, Kandinsky, Klee, Manet, Matisse, Miró, Mondrian, Picasso, Sisley, Tzara, Van Gogh and Warhol – all are artists I most revere. Acquired by Braintree Museum and Art Gallery

Real Artists Do Make Textiles
90 x 109cm (35½ x 43in)
My mother passed away just after I finished making *Real Artists Don't Make Textiles*. This work was made as a follow-on and in dedication to Mam, who was a multi-talented artist and pianist; her photograph is featured in the central panel. Acquired by Braintree Museum and Art Gallery.

CONCEPTS AND INFLUENCES

I believe it was Picasso who once defined all art as being abstract because it can never be perfectly realistic. When we study the work of Mondrian, Kandinsky and some of the other great artists, it is interesting to note how often their paintings evolved from fairly traditional and unexceptional beginnings. Initially many of these artists worked quite conventionally and painted landscapes, still lifes and so on, but increasingly – as they confronted all the usual challenges in painting and began to experiment with different concepts and approaches – they produced images that were decidedly abstract in content. This is similar to my own experience, and I believe that this sort of foundation and natural development gives the work strength and integrity.

Looking at a wide range of abstract painting – preferably examples in galleries, rather than reproductions in books – and getting to understand the various approaches and techniques involved in creating them are obviously useful ways of gaining a broader experience and appreciation of abstract qualities. As you embrace these qualities in your own work, the direction that you take might be influenced and inspired by the paintings of other artists. See *Cover Girl* (below) for an example of this. I have always been a huge fan of Vincent van Gogh; I love his brilliant use of colour, his innovative brush strokes and the emotional impact of his paintings, and this has had a great influence on my own use of colour. Van Gogh's theories of art are quoted in lines written in a letter to his brother Theo: 'Real painters do not paint things as they are… They paint them as they themselves feel them to be.'

Cover Girl (detail)
71 x 53cm (28 x 21in)
Inspired by comic strip illustrations and the work of Roy Lichtenstein.

AN IMPROVISED EMPHASIS

Improvisation and the abstract method distance themselves from conventional teaching methods, which are generally concerned only with developing technical skills and reflecting reality. Instead, it is instinct and the willingness to trust it that now comes into play. As counterintuitive as it seems, intuition involves countless subjective considerations and small judgments – not rational judgments or evaluations, but intuitive decisions, each one propelling the work beyond its limits. This method of working moves away from the use of step-by-step examples, which is a procedure that, although having some value, is in essence a considerable obstacle to the development of artistry and creativity. If you want more than technical perfection, you must first of all concentrate on developing your artistic and intuitive skills. So to follow the abstract method, start with the source: your hidden talent.

Colour Block
Each block measures 30 x 30 x 2.5cm (12 x 12 x 1in)
I'm interested in the interaction between colours and therefore constantly play with different arrangements of pattern, shape and colour.

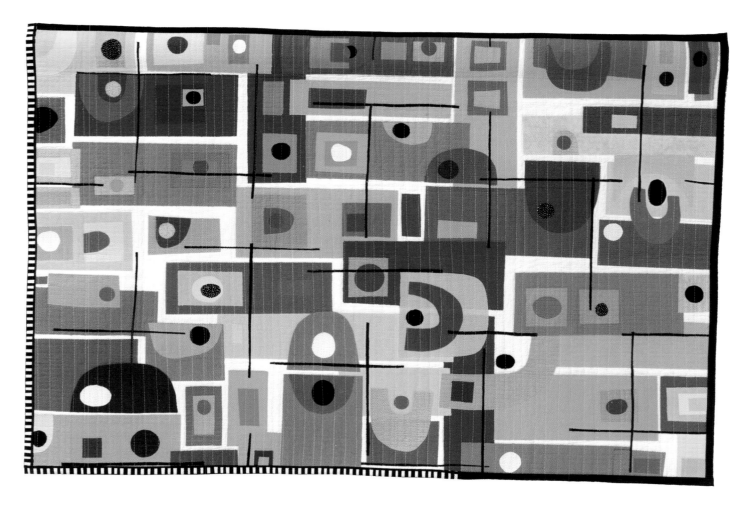

When you are working directly from a subject, on the basis of reproducing what is seen and registered, the starting point for any composition is to make decisions about the format, content and aims for the work. Usually the subject matter is comprised of many different elements of interest: a rhythm of shapes, the pattern of light and dark, reflections, textures and so on. An absolutely essential skill in creating improvised art quilts is being able to view the subject matter as a sequence of shapes, rather than a series of specific objects. You also have to distance yourself from the accepted norm of subject or background. Train yourself to look beyond the obvious and to notice associations and relationships.

Just as shapes can be simplified, emphasized or interpreted in a certain way, so can colours. Often it is best to restrict the colour range and perhaps exploit differences in colour intensities and characteristics. Remember that colours have an emotive quality and therefore the choice and balance of colours invariably has a profound effect on our reaction to a quilt or artwork. Another important factor to consider, and one that is sometimes misjudged, is the size and shape of a work. Try working the same subject on a small scale in multiples and then as a single on a large scale, or in both vertical and horizontal formats, and you will see how this influences the finished results. For an example of this, see *Vertical Lines* on page 45.

Colour Composition
61 x 122cm (24 x 48in)
This piece is concerned with colour and spaces, shapes and forms. Fabrics have been cut and fused to interpret the movement and juxtaposition of simple forms.

EXERCISE 2: USING VERTICAL LINES

This exercise uses plain fabric to create an improvised block based on *Vertical Lines* (opposite). The layered lines add a diagonal emphasis to the composition. These instructions are for a basic 45 × 45cm (18 × 18in) block.

Materials and equipment

- 45 × 45cm (18 × 18in) each of plain cotton, iron-on medium weight interfacing, wadding (batting) or interlining, and calico (muslin) for the backing
- A selection of pre-fused plain colour cotton fabrics
- Fusible webbing or Bondaweb (Wonder Under), to heat-fuse fabrics together
- Sharp scissors or a rotary cutter, mat and acrylic ruler (whichever you prefer working with)
- Iron and ironing board
- Greaseproof (bakery) paper to protect your iron and board when fusing fabrics
- Pressing cloth and spray gun
- Sewing machine
- Assorted machine embroidery threads (floss)

Method

1. Prepare your foundation background by ironing the rough side of the interfacing to the wrong side of the plain fabric square.
2. Collect an assortment of pre-fused fabrics into matching long and short lengths. Take your scissors or rotary cutter and free cut these into five 45cm (18in) long strips. Repeat until you have more than enough strips to cover the background. Sort the strips into piles of the same colour and store in plastic envelopes – you can keep the leftovers for future projects.
3. Place your plain cotton background square, right side up, on an ironing board or working surface. Peel the backing papers off the strips and start to cover the background, placing the pieces right side up and rough side down. Layer in a sequence of the largest down first; overlap with the medium and finish with the smallest.
4. Use your eye to place and layer the colours and work from the centre to the outer edges. Periodically cover the

design with greaseproof (bakery) paper and hot press to anchor the shapes as you layer.
5. Use your imagination when placing the strips: scatter, overlap, or leave spaces to allow the background to show through.
6. Once you are satisfied with the placement, cover with a cloth, spray and press with a hot iron so that the design is firmly anchored into position.
7. To prepare for stitching, place the calico (muslin) backing right side down, add the layer of wadding (batting) or interlining, then place the collage on top right side up. Pin the layers together.
8. Stitch randomly through the layers a multitude of times, using a straight stitch and a variety of coloured threads (floss) and taking the pins out as you go. Repeat this process until the background is stitched to your satisfaction, making sure you have covered any raw edges.
9. Finally, press again and trim any thread ends. The block is now ready to be turned into a cushion, a small hanging or used as part of a larger scale quilt.

Vertical Lines
Each block measures 44 x 33cm (17 x 13in)
This composition came about from a spontaneous play of line. Sometimes it is more effective to restrict the colour range and take advantage of differences in colour intensities and characteristics.

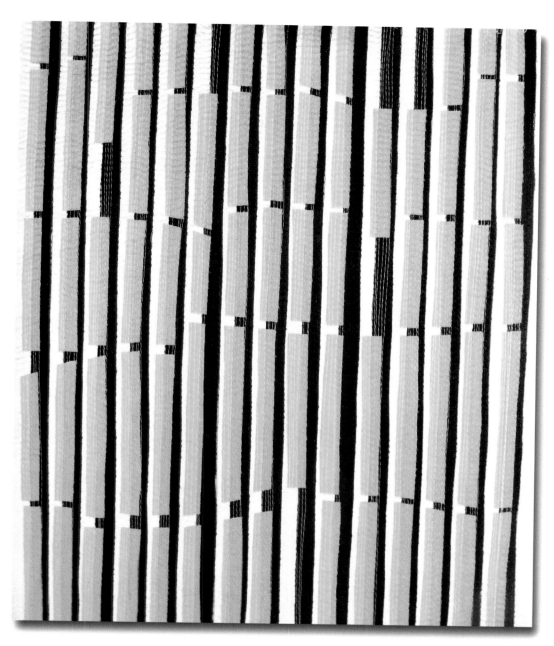

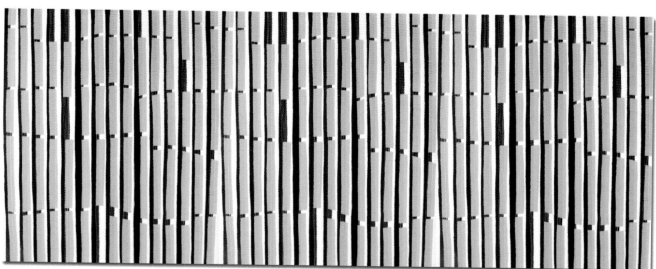

3 INSPIRATION AND INTUITION

BECOMING A QUILT ARTIST

As a quilt artist you need to have technical skills, painting skills, artistic skills and expressive skills. Together these form the nucleus of any artistic process, regardless of style. A great number of quilt-making courses are on offer, but artistic skills are seldom specifically included in the teaching programme. The abstract method of improvised quilt-making is therefore specifically directed towards the activation, stimulation, development and broadening of our artistic qualities and our internal emotions. To learn to work from within yourself, from your inner nature, is therefore the first step.

Creativity, expression, colour and individuality are key elements when working with improvisation. These four qualities are the essential practice of creating art and are therefore also the starting point and the aim of abstract improvisation. In other words your goal is not to make a magnificent work of art immediately, but to first study and develop your artistic skills – the most important requirement in order to be able to accomplish 'art'. The stimulus for designing this alternative method was the realization that qualities such as one's own contribution and artistic appreciation are often neglected. Because of this, many works give the impression of being clumsy or crude, which need not happen if we were less concerned about a satisfactory result and paid more attention to the essential skills and qualities we require as quilt artists. So, if your goal is to experience new ways of making quilts, then embrace the improvised process by using your intuition and work spontaneously. The quilt *Spotaholic* (shown opposite) is a good example of this.

Motivations for improvisation

• Improvisation stimulates experimentation, discovery, creativity and the activation of your talent.
• Improvised abstraction is the ideal opportunity not to follow the traditional and accepted, but instead to strike out entirely on your own path and to develop your own style. It paves the way for originality and individuality.
• To work instinctively invokes abilities such as feeling, intuition, inventiveness, spontaneity, feeling for shape, colour, composition, harmony… These abilities form the basis of every pure, creative and artistic expression.
• Even if you do not have any drawing, painting or stitching experience you can learn the expressive abstract method without knowing any complicated techniques.
• If you prefer to continue working representatively, abstraction remains the ideal way to reproduce reality according to your own interpretation.
• Improvisation allows you to escape from merely reproducing 'pictures' or examples, and having total freedom of action adds an extra dimension to your experience of quilt-making.
• In order to make your own judgement, you simply have to try and experience.

Spotaholic
51 x 51cm (20 x 20in)
One of a series made by using randomly cut small circles of hand-painted cotton to create a textured surface. The pieces are enhanced by adding appliqué spots to the background of each circle, creating a multitude of coloured circles in various combinations.

SUBJECT MATTER

Quilt design can be approached in many ways and the assignments in this book work well for all who are new to working instinctively. You will need to experiment to find the way that works best for you; whatever way you choose, it is up to you to explore pattern, shape, and colour in new ways, think with your gut feeling and embrace the process of working intuitively. If you prefer to invent ideas and work spontaneously by using an abstract approach, your choice of subject matter will be extensive. Any subject can be interpreted in an abstract way, but for anyone new to this style of working I would suggest that simple, uncomplicated shapes make the best starting point. Finding the right shapes to use, deciding on the best colour relationships and so on is never easy. But there are devices, exercises and techniques that can help. For example, viewing a subject through half-closed eyes will help you to focus on the main shapes, rather than seeing unnecessary details.

The quilts of Swiss quilt artist Marianne Häni (shown right), are very often inspired by nature, music and her inner feelings. She says: 'My work is about expressing my inner feelings and my reaction to nature, music, works of painters, sculptors, designers and many other sources of inspiration. They do not usually bear a political or other deeper message, they are meant to draw the eye of the viewer and to touch his sense of harmony. My work is always about colour – I like clear, strong and pure colours. I am often going back to the traditional shape of the square and the rectangle in all their dimensions, but I also like to break out and use freely cut, organic lines. Dense machine quilting is often used to give the work an additional and sometimes completely new structure.'

One way of arriving at a satisfactory design for a quilt is to make a sequence of small blocks, as illustrated in *Sticks 'n'*

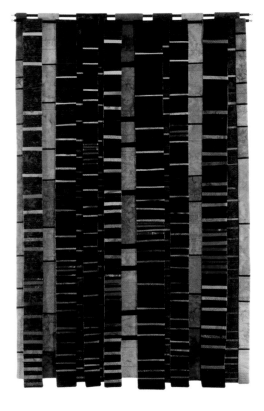

Good Vibrations
Marianne Häni
130 x 80cm (51 x 31½ in)
For this quilt Marianne asked her son, who is a jazz musician, to tell her what came to his mind when he heard the title of this piece of music. His answer was 'a lot of bright green vibrating stripes on a dark background'.

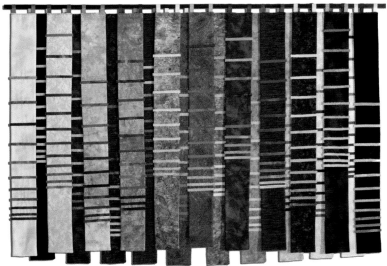

Colour Play
Marianne Häni
112 x 160cm (44 x 63in)
As a child, and even now, Marianne loved to arrange the coloured pencils in her pencil box – it inspired her to make this work consisting of 21 individual narrow panels.

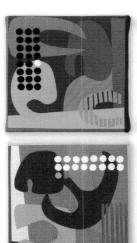

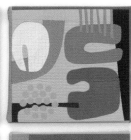

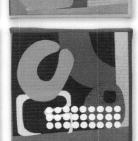

Colour Cube
91.5 x 120 x 2.5cm
(36 x 47 x 1in)
This collage is based on horizontal and vertical lines, combining curves and circles within the design. Most of my preparatory work is done while spontaneously playing with shape and colour, checking the proportions and other essential qualities as the design progresses.

Stones (see page 14), *Colour Block* (see page 43), and *Colour Cube* (shown above). Having made the first block, simplify or modify it further as you make the second and carry on in this fashion until you have the right balance of shapes and other qualities that you need. Try out the exercise techniques to make small samples and then keep these samples handy to refer to later, or finish them into small works of art by mounting on artist stretchers.
I believe it is good to present finished works as professionally as possible, and with this in mind have included some ideas on unconventional finishing in chapter 1 (see page 29).

Thin Blue Line (detail)
61 x 81cm (24 x 32in)
This piece was inspired by movement and colour – and a hat I was making at the time.

Inspiration

Inspiration is the best word to use for a collection of ideas. New places are a great source of inspiration, even if it is just a trip to the village shop, or seeing a display in a shop window or decorative art on a building. As a nature lover, I find ideas all around – landscape, rural or urban, is full of inspiration; you never know what might catch your eye.

Digital images and photographs are also a useful source of inspiration; looking at and taking your own photographs is a great starting point. The information gathered from one image might well inspire a number of different quilts – and remember that the negative spaces in a subject can be just as interesting and important as the positive shapes. When taking shots, instead of just pointing the camera and taking the picture, think about making pleasing compositions and about how you are framing the subject matter. Look at the photograph and think about the elements and how you want to use them in your work.

If you are not yet ready to work freely, you may find it helpful to put tracing paper over the photo and trace the main design lines. You cannot see insignificant details through the tracing paper, so this will help you see the composition that you were initially drawn to in simple terms. Remember that the elements you are attracted to in the photograph do not have to stay in the same position in the composition. The purpose of abstraction is not to make an image exactly the same as the photo – if that were the case, you would be making appliqué.

Image sources for inspiration: use examples of nature, architecture and landscape to motivate your creative process and initiate ideas. Clockwise from top left: tree bark; plant bark; threads; the sky; playground railings; a castor oil plant; a rose; branches.

Art books and magazines are another source of material that can both inspire and be used in your work. Old pattern books and retro fabric designs are also excellent attention-grabbers that can lead to a striking palette and lots of ideas. Try looking objectively at what you are seeing, rather than just focusing, and you will find colour combinations that capture your attention. Give yourself challenges and work with colours that are out of your comfort zone – learn to see colour in a new way and embrace the challenge of using it instinctively.

Within the works of Welsh textile artist Alison Moger (shown right), there are fragments of the past that are often humorous and cathartic, but always beautiful. She has continued to be inspired by her natural surroundings and her work reflects on family life and her Welsh roots.

Up the Garden 1 and 2
(right)
Alison Moger
32 x 32cm (12 x 12in)
Alison Moger: 'These stitched pieces are based on my memories of helping in the garden and allotments as a child, with the use of recycled and vintage fabrics evoking the character of the valley garden and proudly owned allotment. Each greenhouse was constructed from found wood and pieces salvaged from the colliery; there was no such thing as a bought greenhouse. I loved being involved in this activity and to this day warm memories are evoked when I see an old garden shed or allotments from the roadside.'

STANDARD BASICS –
THE INTUITIVE TOOLBOX

It is not essential to have a variety of tools and techniques in your workbox to work intuitively. Whether you are a beginner or an accomplished quilter you can focus on executing exciting new designs using few materials and simple techniques. There is no better way to learn than by doing, so with this in mind I have kept my advice and directions to a minimum. I want you to think of my guidance simply as a collection of strategic tips given to someone who already knows what to do. You have your own innate artistic intuition to guide you, but it's up to you to supply the passion to make things and the hunger to try out myriad possibilities in your art in order for it to succeed.

Let us look to see what you will need to start working instinctively. Of course when making a quilt or collage we layer, paint, print and stitch cloth, but when working instinctively the artist's 'tools' need to include more. As when making any form of artwork we can roughly divide these 'tools' into a number of elements, or abstract values.

We can differentiate these elements into three categories:

Primary representation: pattern, shape, colour, size, line, tone, texture.
Composition: formation, arrangement, structure.
Secondary representation: design, movement, repetition, balance, harmony, variation, emphasis, contrast, depth, space, division.

Every work is an arrangement, structuring, merging or composition of parts of these elements. If we consciously pay attention to these elements in the course of our study we will learn to recognize them and adjust our imagery. And the more experience we have with this, the stronger our skills will

become; in the long run, we will be able to use these artistic sources of feeling both freely and intuitively, which is why these elements are the starting point in improvised quilt-making.

In her *Structure* series (shown below and opposite), the American textile artist Lisa Call investigates the boundaries we use to divide our world, exploring human-made structures for containment such as fences and stone walls. Lines of posts, negative space created between odd-shaped stones, and uniform rows of bricks are all of interest. As the series matured her focus shifted to the psychological barriers humans use to protect themselves emotionally, exploring how we hide our true thoughts and feelings with imagined roadblocks.

Structure #116 *(right)*
Lisa Call
86 x 104cm (34 x 41in)
The *Structure* series investigates the boundaries we use to divide our world. It explores both physical fences and walls and abstract, psychological barriers used for emotional protection.

Structure #97 *(below; detail shown below left)*
Lisa Call
71 x 117cm (28 x 46in)
Lisa creates bold geometric and contemporary textile paintings composed of her own richly coloured, hand-dyed fabric. Her work is abstract but draws elements from many places: her love of the colours and geological forms of the south-west, repetition, pattern, and an attraction to human-made structures for containment, such as fences and stone walls.

DEPTH AND SPACE

In pure abstract work that relies on the use of formal elements such as line, shape and colour, quilt artists often only exploit the idea of flat space or conceptual space. For example, where the design of a piece is based on a sequence of coloured shapes, all of which are designed with flat colour, there may be no attempt to convey an illusion of depth. Instead, most likely the emphasis will be on the interaction of the colours, lines and shapes to create contrasts and a rhythm of balance and tension in the work. Since depth and space are not essential qualities – unlike in representational work – it is not necessary to consider aspects such as a focal point; abstract collage can be multifocal.

In some instances the play of colours and shapes can produce an effective illusion of space, even if this is not 'real' space in the sense that we cannot relate it to specific objects and points of reference. See *Rhosyn Coch* (shown right), for example. Another instance of this would be Op Art, in which some lines and shapes may appear to jump forward while others recede. In fact 'conceptual' space of this type may occur quite unintentionally, because the brain automatically wants to understand things as being three-dimensional rather than two-dimensional.

In representational and semi-abstract work an element of pictorial space is usually essential. Spatial perception is one of the more difficult aspects of quilt-making; from cave art to modern times artists and makers have devised various ways of depicting a convincing feeling of three-dimensional form and space, despite the obvious limitations of a two-dimensional surface. For an example of this see the *Twigs* quilt (page 83).

Rhosyn Coch - Red Rose
122 x 203cm (48 x 80in)
A red rose represents love and that is why I have used it as the main source of inspiration in this piece of work. There is an inference of light and shade in the piece, which naturally adds to the sense of space.

MAKING ARTISTIC DECISIONS

When undertaking any new work, the process from the initial idea to the final stitch inevitably involves numerous decisions. The chief factor in making most, if not all, of these decisions is the artist's perception or understanding in response to what is seen and felt as the work develops. For some artists these decisions are made rationally and objectively, and result from careful consideration of the subject matter and the work in progress. The work of American quilt artist Terry Jarrard-Dimond (shown below and opposite) can originate as a response to a colour, a song or something she has read; all her pieces are combinations of things she experiences in daily living. She says of her work: 'The evocative power of compositions created from abstract or non-objective shapes drives the development of my art. My work is constructed from my own hand-dyed fabric and is created in a way that utilizes both preparatory sketches and/or improvisational techniques. I refer to my pieces as interior landscapes. These landscapes are often filled with figures, structures and vistas that have a story to tell but which are very open to interpretation.'

For other artists the approach is a more instinctive one, and, although still influenced by their senses and other factors, the decisions are taken quickly and seemingly without conscious reasoning. There are different levels and aspects of perception, but however inexperienced you are, it is impossible to make quilts without some awareness of the basic elements, such as colour, line, shape and form. In time, as we gain experience, we recognize that each decision we take when working is influenced by what has already been achieved in the piece. The marks we make and the colours we use are always relative to their context. And in turn, these marks help to determine what comes next.

Consequently, perception is a quality that is important throughout the quilt-making process. Initially, decisions have to be made about the general aims and content of the work; thereafter, to fulfil those objectives, a sensitive use of colour, technique and other aspects of quilt-making and visual language are vital at every stage.

Steppin' Out *(right)*
Terry Jarrard-Dimond
152.5 x 120cm (60¼ x 47in)
The artist's inspiration for *Steppin' Out* began with a desire to incorporate strip piecing into a composition. As it evolved, however, each piece was cut individually in relation to the one before.

The Big Red Dog *(below)*
Terry Jarrard-Dimond
97 x 115.5cm (38¼ x 45½in)
This work began as an abstract composition, but the 'dog' found his way into it and was allowed to stay. Terry has been drawn to the making of art all of her remembered life – she feels most in her element in the studio, her thoughts and hands working together in the creation of her art.

USING SKETCHBOOKS

I believe that there is no such thing as a 'bad' drawing in a sketchbook. The primary value of the drawings and notes you put into your sketchbook is to inspire new ideas to work on without worrying about whether any particular drawing looks 'good' or is a 'finished' piece. In other words, it's important to feel comfortable with the casualness of your sketchbook and not to feel intimidated by the notion that someone may look at it and see a poor rendering or a scribble they don't understand. With this in mind, your sketchbooks should contain only the simplest of drawings, such as plain, outlined contours that are free of elaborate details and unnecessary embellishments of colour, value and texture. Think of your sketchbook as a practical tool that helps you bank your ideas and spontaneous

flashes of inspiration so that you can use them for future reference. In order for your sketchbook to function properly, you need to keep an open mind about the value of visual ideas that come to you without any forethought or planning. Your sketchbook can then be the place where anything goes and where you don't have to be overly concerned about what anything looks like. Basically you just use your sketchbook to jot down new ideas.

I recommend that you start keeping a simple sketchbook from the beginning, as an ongoing part of your art-making. Instead of using an expensive commercial art shop sketchbook, I would recommend that you use simple, blank, A4 (letter) paper, stored in a loose-leaf file. I prefer copier paper and a file because it is cheap, available anywhere and easy to use.

Suburbia (above)
**132 x 168cm x 2.5cm
(52 x 66 x 1in)**
The colours used in *Suburbia* came out of the trials and tribulations experienced while moving from the hustle and bustle and sheer buzz of inner city living to the peaceful tranquility, bird song (and boredom…) of suburbia.

Getting started with your sketchbook

The first step when starting your sketchbook is to decide what you want to do with it and how you can make it serve your artistic needs. Here are some suggestions for ways to make your sketchbook most useful:

• Plan on a regular routine of working, and commit to it.
• Think of every drawing in your sketchbook as being disposable. Jot down ideas or rough drawings for future quilts, collages, prints or other projects. Make handwritten notes to record details and ideas that are too difficult to draw.
• Use your sketchbook to make spontaneous drawings (doodles) that have no predetermined subject. Record ideas that come to you in a dream or just seem to appear out of the blue.
• Use your sketchbook to keep materials like colour swatches, texture samples, photographs or collage materials for future projects.
• Your sketchbook can also be a good place to write down notes to yourself about any topics that relate to your art, or to your creative process, or writing down self-critiques about what you think of your own work (what you like about it and what you don't like about it). You could also note comments others have made about your art that may be useful to think about.
• Use it to keep a note on how well you are doing at using your intuition, working spontaneously or keeping up with your work schedule.

Keeping a portfolio

I strongly recommend that you keep much of the work you create from the exercises in this book in three separate boxes or portfolios, labelled 'Like', 'Dislike' and 'TBC' (To Be Continued).

• The purpose of the Like and Dislike portfolios is to keep examples of work you consider to be your best and worst attempts at a particular exercise for the valuable knowledge you can gain by comparing these two extremes. They will give you a critical perspective on your work that is lost when you only keep those things that you like. It's also true that you stand to learn more from the pieces that you don't like.
• The TBC portfolio contains examples of sketches, drawings or samples that you may want to continue developing at another time or use to inspire other work.
• Another possibility for this portfolio is to use portions of these works (interesting sections) in future collages and assemblage artworks.
• The portfolios are a record of your ideas and development as an artist. All the work you keep there – the good, the bad and the ugly – is an important part of your creative expression. Don't underestimate your abilities, or be quick to throw away potentially valuable resources that might feed your imagination and provide ideas for future work.
• A portfolio can also help you answer the oft-asked question, 'What do I want to work on today?'
• The size of the box or portfolio should be large enough to hold 20 to 30 examples of your work. You can construct a portfolio yourself by getting two pieces of plain A3 cardboard and using duct tape to put them together; or buy the cheapest ones you can find at an art shop. Ikea is also a good source for cheap plastic boxes.

EXERCISE 3: USING PLAIN AND PAINTED FABRICS

This exercise is to create an improvised block based on the *Any Colour You Like* deconstructed quilt (shown opposite). These instructions are for a basic 30 × 30cm (12 × 12in) block.

Materials and equipment

- 30 × 30cm (12 × 12in) each of plain black cotton, iron-on medium weight interfacing, wadding (batting) or interlining, and calico (muslin) for the backing
- A selection of pre-fused plain and interesting painted fabrics – use your own painted fabrics
- Sharp scissors
- Iron and ironing board
- Greaseproof (bakery) paper to protect your iron and board when fusing fabrics
- Pressing cloth and spray gun
- Sewing machine
- Assorted machine embroidery threads (floss)

Method

1. Prepare your background panel by ironing the rough side of the interfacing to the wrong side of the black fabric.
2. Select a collection of pre-fused fabrics. Take your scissors and free cut these into assorted large-size squares and oblongs, smaller spirals, circular cutouts and other stylized shapes. Cut enough to cover the background panel.
3. Place your background panel, right side up, on an ironing board or working surface. Arrange and scatter the shapes until you find a layout you like, allowing the black background to show through in places. Peel the backing paper from the shapes and layer them right side up, rough side down. Add spirals, circular cutouts and other stylized shapes on top.
4. Periodically cover the design with the greaseproof (bakery) paper, and hot press to anchor the shapes as you work.
5. Once you are satisfied with the placement, cover with a cloth, spray and press with a hot iron so that the design is firmly anchored into position.
6. To prepare for stitching, place the calico (muslin) backing right side down, add the layer of wadding (batting) or interlining and then place the collage on top, right side up. Pin the layers together.
7. Stitch randomly through the layers a multitude of times, using a straight stitch and a variety of coloured threads (floss), and taking the pins out as you go. Repeat this process until the background is stitched to your satisfaction, making sure you have covered any raw edges.
8. Finally, press again and trim any thread ends. The panel is now ready for stretching onto a wooden frame.
9. To make a deconstructed quilt like *Any Colour You Like*, repeat the process to make a further five panels, merging the panels by carrying and repeating individual shapes across the surface.

***Any Colour You Like*
(detail)
Each block 30 x 30cm
(12 x 12in)**
In this deconstructed art quilt the blocks (only one of which is shown here) have been made from free-cut shapes using fabric offcuts from other projects. A madcap assortment of shapes randomly applied form the basis for this quilt.

4 COLOUR, COMPOSITION AND SURFACE EFFECTS

THE IMPACT OF COLOUR

Both in improvised and abstract work the element of colour is a major component and source of inspiration and expression. Colour is more than a superficial observation registered by the eye, since receiving colour signals triggers the creation of a special kind of communication in which our emotions play a major role. Colour does something to us. Because we instinctively accept and value certain colours and reject and dismiss others, it is often our feeling for colour that determines whether a work of art affects us or not. For an artist colour is, as it were, the messenger of a certain emotion, mood, atmosphere, aim or involvement. Colour speaks, tells our story, seeks contact with the onlooker and gives atmosphere and character to our work. The impact of colour is therefore far wider than just registering attractive colour planes and shapes, so it is important to develop our feeling for colour in order to make full use of this expressive pictorial element.

Most artists are aware of colour theory and the colour wheel, a useful visual aid that explains variations of hue and tone. Knowing what complementary colours are, and also how to use colour, is useful for everyone, whether you are making art or just looking at it, and can enable us all to appreciate more fully the effect of colour in both art and daily life. Be adventurous in your choice of colours by putting unexpected combinations together. I often add black and white and combine vivid with pastel arrangements, as seen in the *Yin and Yang* quilt (see below and opposite) – Yin is black and Yang white. The quilt was inspired by Chinese philosophy and the concept that the yin is feminine, earth, water, coldness and so on and is related to fate. The yang is masculine, heaven, fire, heat and so on and is connected to free will. Neither is good or bad – according to Daoism, everyone contains both yin and yang. Whenever there is less of one there is more of the other. We need to strive to keep them both in balance.

Yin and Yang
122 x 122cm (48 x 48in)
Inspired by the traditional Chinese philosophy of Yin and Yang. According to legend, the Chinese emperor Fu Hsi claimed that the best state for everything in the universe is a state of harmony represented by a balance of yin and yang.

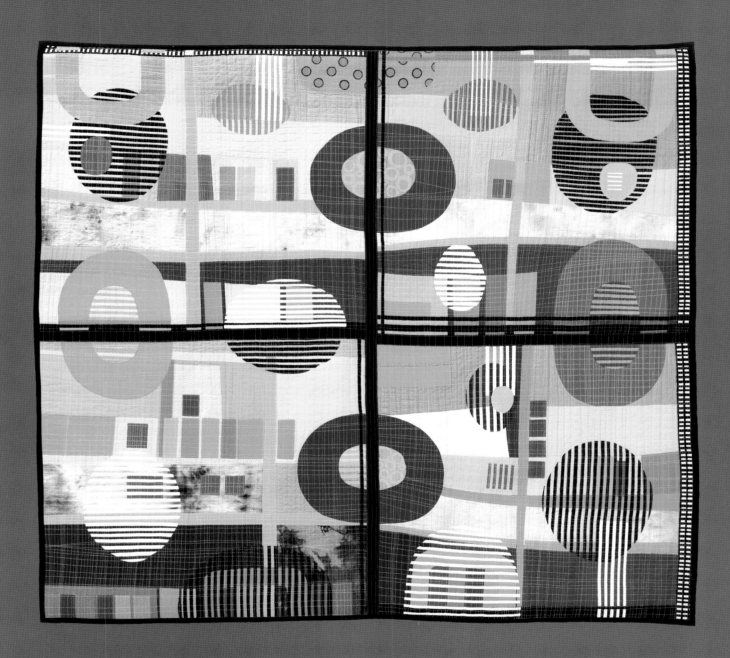

USING COLOUR

I believe that the most successful colour combinations come from risk-taking, and while colour may work technically, it may work more successfully on an emotional level – we should follow our gut instinct rather than sticking only to colour theory. It is important to experiment and use different materials to explore combinations of colour and variations of tonal qualities. Gradually using colour will become instinctive, based not on theory but on personal experience, and how we use colour can be both inspiring and liberating.

One of the most interesting things about working with colour is that while light influences colour and often creates great drama and impact in a composition, it is colour that provides the means to interpret such effects. In every idea where contrast is a significant feature and consideration, the logical starting point is to examine the shades of colour you are using and how this influences the character and mood of the finished piece. For example, the shades may be subdued, stark, warm or cool – each type of shade will radically influence the look and feel of the design. In addition, the strength and direction of the contrasts are likely to create tonal variations within areas of colour, helping to define objects that produce interesting combinations. For an example of this see the piece *Light Fall* (see page 66) by English quilt artist Janet Twinn. Janet says of her work: 'I have always been interested in grids and patterns, particularly the invisible patterns that underpin the structure of life itself. Much of my work is constructed around a grid, I like the way it mirrors the warp and weft of the cloth. This is the formal part of my practice. I like having this framework in which to play with colour. *Light Fall* is part of a series of work that explores the effects of colour illuminated by light. Painting with dye for me is an intuitive process; although past experience is a

Un, Dau, Tri (above)
112 x 198cm (44 x 79in)
The second in a series of six works inspired by my love of graffiti as an art form, coupled with my interest in the decline and revival of the Welsh language. The printed words used in the quilt refer to the Welsh translation of the English names for the colours: *coch* = red, *glas* = blue, and so on.

guide to what to expect from certain combinations of colours, there is always an element of surprise.'

I use colour to express my thoughts and feelings. Moreover – because I believe it is important to make a personal, emotional response rather than to be constrained by an objective, representational approach – I am not afraid to select, simplify, distort or use whatever devices are necessary to interpret my idea. It should be stressed that elements such as colour cannot be considered in isolation. Essentially, the impact and ultimate success of an art quilt depends on the degree of emphasis given to colour, line, shape, pattern, rhythm, composition and so on. See *Un, Dau, Tri* (above); the Welsh words are those for the colours used in the triptych, and the shapes and text flow naturally from one panel to the next, creating relationships and atmosphere between the individual shapes and compositions and making these elements interdependent.

Colour is everywhere and is something for all of us to enjoy, but we tend to take it for granted: how often do we look at a flower or landscape, for instance, and really analyse our response to it? Colour is very personal, and individual tastes vary enormously: what is warm and appealing to one person may be dull and dreary to another. And it is certainly true that a like or dislike of particular colours and response to particular colour combinations changes throughout life, affected by environment, fashion and other external factors. There is a sheer delight in putting colours together and seeing the effects they create. Joy, despair, anger – all emotion can be expressed with colour – as seen in *Black Hole – Mourning Quilt* (see page 69).

I WANT TO STITCH –

ART QUILTS

DEFINED BY PATTERN SHAPE AND COLOUR

VIEWED AS ART BY ART COLLECTORS

I WANT TO STITCH QUILTS

AS A REFLECTION OF OUR PAST

IMPARTING CONTEXT AND VALUES

TEAR MEND MUSE LAYER FUSE QUILT

QUILTS USING RECYCLED MATERIALS AS

A MEDIUM FOR ADDRESSING POLITICAL

AND SOCIAL ISSUES

I WANT TO STITCH 1000 WHITE TEEPEES

AS A TESTAMENT TO LOVE NOT WAR

THOUGHTS THAT LIE TOO DEEP FOR TEARS

QUILTS THAT STIMULATE MY PEERS

I WANT TO STITCH – QUILTS

THAT ARE WORTH MORE THAN GOLD

THAT KEEP THE HOMELESS WARM

THAT SWATHE A NEW BORN BABE

THAT BRING BACK MEMORIES

THAT ARE HERE WHEN I AM GONE

I WANT TO STITCH

QUILTS

Positively Negative
80 x 90cm
(31½ x 35½in)
Inspiration for this piece
came from negative
comments and how they
can overpower a positive
outlook. Using a 'plus sign'
as a motif, it conveys a
happy, positive attitude
about life in general. The
bright red appliquéd text
serves to add sparks to
represent all of the
wonderful things we can
each experience if we
maintain a positive
attitude.

ASSESSING IDEAS

It is always exciting to be inspired by an
idea that you instinctively want to create.
However, somehow that initial euphoria
must be matched by the skills required to
convert inspiration into a successful work.
Spontaneity is an essential quality when
making art quilts, but, on the other hand,
starting work without some idea as to the
general content and objectives may well
prove disastrous. It is a question of finding
the right balance between planning what
you wish to express and the way you
intend to express it, and allowing yourself
the freedom to modify things and consider
other ideas as the work develops. Quilt-
making should never rely on the same tried
and tested approach. Inevitably this results
in work that lacks vitality and originality,
and it stifles creative development. Each

new work requires something different.
Similarly, there is no advantage in only
making quilts that you feel confident with
and that you know will succeed.

The challenge of improvisation will keep
your work lively and interesting, at the
same time adding to your skills and
experience. In my initial assessment of an
idea I generally consider which aspects are
the most important and roughly how I will
interpret these in the work, the type of
colour and – if the work is inspired by a
statement or poem – the design and size of
the wording itself, how it will be
appropriate to the size and shape of the
finished quilt. In the piece *Positively
Negative* (shown above), colours have been
used to depict the feelings of negative and
positive thoughts.

Gardens and flowers are a favourite source of ideas; they present a wealth of inspiration for colourful formations and offer scope for both the specific and the general view. Compositions can include buildings or parts of buildings, garden furniture, ponds, ornaments and other decorative features. Normally the composition is as effective as the original – I look for a strong design in which colour will play a key role.

Black Hole – Mourning Quilt (detail)
142 x 122cm (56 x 48in)
This quilt represents how I felt at the time when my much-loved parents and family passed away. I sometimes like to work with direct reference to the subject matter, as this allows me to select and use whatever colours best suit the piece as it develops.

Landscape and the structure and grouping of buildings, such as those shown in *Tiger Bay Reinvented* (below), can give a very interesting pattern of shapes and colours from which to design a quilt or collage. I also find holiday brochures and snapshots inspiring – such views offer much scope for bold compositions and expressive colour. For example, in *A Place in the Sun* (right) I have mainly used different tones of sunny, warm yellows and greens to suggest the feeling of the hot exterior.

Bathing Huts (left)
61 x 61cm (24 x 24in)
The design of this piece was inspired by photographs of bathing huts.

Tiger Bay Reinvented
(detail) (left)
99 x 127cm (39 x 50in)
Inspired by the Cardiff Bay new development of old Tiger Bay, the balance of colours and geometric shapes of the buildings worked out well. I have tried to focus on how I feel about the development, rather than aiming for a detailed description that shows every architectural feature.

A Place in the Sun
61 x 30cm (24 x 12in)
This piece was inspired by a holiday brochure.

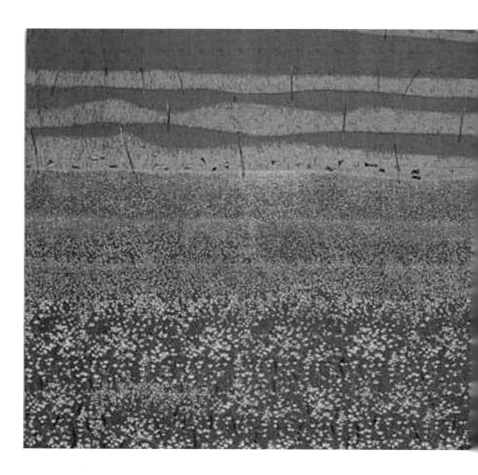

Landscape is the main inspiration for English quilt artist Elizabeth Brimelow. She is interested in how history has shaped her native landscape; its fields, woodland, paths and open spaces. And she is also fascinated by marks made on the land, particularly those left by man when planting, harvesting and ploughing. See examples of Elizabeth's work right and below.

Butterland
Elizabeth Brimelow
133.5 x 175.5cm (52½ x 69in)
The field of buttercups that inspired this piece is part of Butterland Farm in the Peak District.

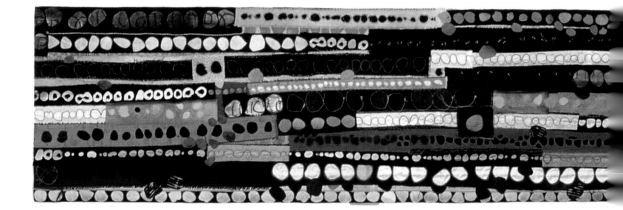

Right: *Shingle*
Elizabeth Brimelow
Two panels, each
54 x 157.5cm
(21¼ x 62in)
These wall panels were inspired by a Suffolk beach.

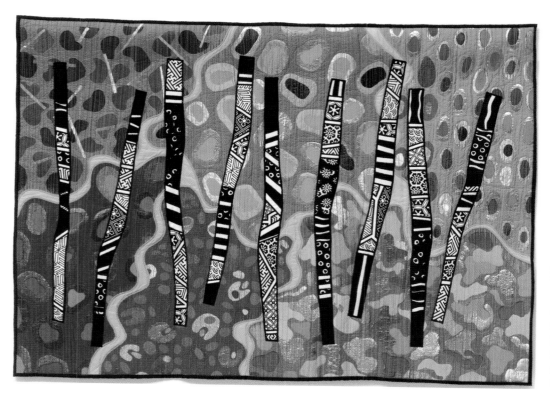

COMPOSITION

Composition is the organisation and arrangement of the pictorial elements and is the framework that gives an artwork an underlying structure and energy. Creating the right balance of shape and colour is never an easy matter, but if the quilt is to be 'read' and understood in the way that we wish, due consideration to the composition is essential. Like so many aspects of quilt-making and other forms of artwork, to begin with – when our confidence and experience is limited – arriving at a satisfactory composition can be a very conscious, contrived process. Gradually it becomes more intuitive, though many artists continue to use thumbnail sketches and other devices to help them resolve the basic composition before they start on the actual work. Like most artists, no doubt my approach to composition is sometimes influenced by different theories or aspects of design that I have noticed in other artists' work. However, I am never really aware of this, so perhaps for me it is a subconscious influence since my judgments about composition tend to be instinctive rather than analytical. Instead of thinking that I ought to use the theoretically most harmonious colour, for example, or that I must avoid placing something exactly in the middle of the painting – because this is supposed to make the composition too balanced – I prefer to choose whatever feels and looks right.

For me, the essential elements of a good composition are rhythm, pattern and colour forms. The shapes and colours should be devised so that they work both independently – related to and inspired by the subject matter – and coherently, so as to generate a rhythm throughout the piece. The composition should create vitality and drama, while at the same time helping the eye travel around the composition and maintaining the viewer's interest within its bounds. The shapes that form the composition can be true to life or they can be simplified or exaggerated in some way, as in *Rain Dance* (shown above). Inevitably, the degree of selection and simplification influences the extent to which the final image appears abstract.

In most of my work the composition is shaped by the needs of the quilt itself, rather than a desire to faithfully interpret the subject matter. While I am working on the composition I am aware of all sorts of considerations: positive and negative shapes, relative space, descriptive and evocative colour and so on. Most of my decisions are made intuitively, but at the back of my mind I know that certain qualities will enhance a composition and others will lessen its impact. For instance I might use an approach that I learned at art college, which is to think of a composition as having four quarters and try to ensure that something different happens in each of these areas – see *Big Top*, above).

Big Top
142 x 122cm (56 x 48in)
A little inspiration from real life and the circus helped to create Big Top, which is full of colourful, energetic and abstract images.

The principle of designing using thirds is something that artists have used since Renaissance times. Based on the Golden Section (or Golden Mean), a proportion that is found in nature and which is generally accepted to create an aesthetically pleasing arrangement, the 'thirds' principle can be applied equally effectively to figurative or abstract work. In the *Juggler* collage (right), a series of simple shapes make up the composition and I have used a division of the picture area that is based on thirds: the foreground fills the lower third and from this I have created a sense of recession through the middle-ground area to the background.

On the other hand, the usual advice is to avoid compositions in which the main elements are symmetrically or evenly balanced, or in which there is an even amount of interest spread throughout the design. Generally speaking, the most successful compositions are those in which there are areas to rest the eye as well as areas of interest. But of course there are really no rules, and other factors, such as colour and texture, can contribute very positively to overall visual impact.

Singularly, you can make immensely effective designs that are based on a diagonal or triangular division of the surface area, using a variety of lines and shapes to lead the eye into and around the work. Again, with composition, as with other aspects of quilt-making, it is good to experiment and so continue to add to your experience and knowledge.

Juggler (detail) (top right)
71 x 56cm (28 x 22in)
Simple shapes using bright colour.

The Bird (right)
71 x 51cm (28 x 20in)
There are various contrasting elements here, each interpreted by using a different medium. For example, choosing collage for the birdcage helps to define it.

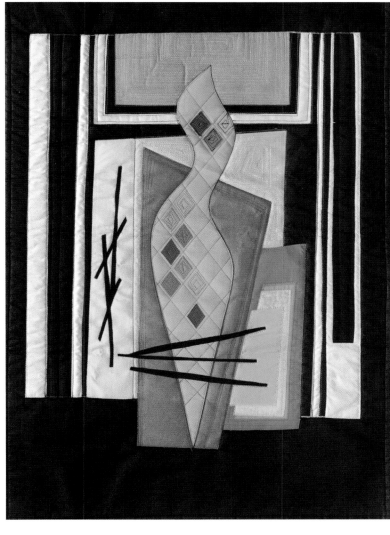

The power of colour

Colour is a dominant expressive device in my work. I enjoy using colour in a bold, confident manner and it is through the considered choice and placing of certain colours that I aim to achieve a particular mood and emotional impact. Moreover, as shown in *Circus Collage* (below), the use of free-cut shapes also conveys a sense of form and space. For example, blocks of flat colour recede into the background, whereas the simple geometric shapes create emphasis and imply proximity.

The fact that I fuse collage, work intuitively and prefer to discover which colours are needed, rather than start with a fixed idea, means of course that I do not work in the conventional way, with a set palette of colours and materials. I regard each work as requiring its own individual colour scheme and technical approach, depending on the mood, impact, particular idea and other qualities that I want to convey. Generally I look for the most influential, dominant colour, which effectively will become the centre of

A Splash of Colour!
(right)
Four panels, each
61 x 61cm (24 x 24in)
My principal concern when making a quilt is colour. Although the subject matter is as important as the principle of the quilt itself, gradually it becomes less significant as the emphasis shifts to composing with colour, shape and form.

Circus Collage – The Juggler, Black Sea Lion, High-wire and White Sea Lion
Four panels, each
61 x 61cm (24 x 24in)
Inspired by the high-wire balancing act at the circus, I was stirred to create a quilt in homage to these brave entertainers. The use of vibrant primary colours was used to set a happy circus mood.

interest in the quilt, and I begin with this. I may decide to use this same colour or, if I think it appropriate, I will change or adjust it, enhance or subdue it by adding differing colour tones. This gives a starting point, and working from this I gradually develop the whole work. As I do so, I am very aware that each new shape and colour will influence and be influenced by those colours already in place. Consequently, in order to achieve the correct colour harmonies and contrasts, colours may have to be adjusted and readjusted as the quilt evolves. The collage series *A Splash of Colour* (above) demonstrates this theory quite well.

EVOKING MOOD

The visual and emotional impact of a work of art is largely dependent on the choice of colours and the interaction of the various colour shapes and intensities across the quilt surface. The most influential factors in defining the strength of this impact are the colour 'key' (whether the colours are warm, cool, neutral, bright and so on) and the way that colour harmonies and contrasts are used. Naturally the effect is more intense in a work where the colour involves striking contrasts and is rich and 'hot', than it is in a work that is subdued in colour. Undoubtedly in my work it is essentially the effect of colour that evokes a particular mood and atmosphere. Expressing the mood through colour is now largely an instinctive process, although one that remains conscious of aspects of colour theory (such as using complementary, analogous, limited or harmonious and integrating colours) to help generate the desired 'feel' and impact of the work. In selecting colours that will contribute to the intended effect it is usually necessary to exaggerate the strength of some, while perhaps understating others.

Been There, Seen It, Done It (right)
122 x 81cm (48 x 32in)
An art quilt inspired by the revival of current fashion trends.

Alt 'a' Vista (below)
99 x 127cm (39 x 50in)
This piece was inspired by change – the changing seasons, the change in my age, circumstances and lifestyle and how I view the future: with a heightened sense of excitement and expectation, anything can happen...

While I am working I always have in mind the narrative of the quilt – the story it is telling – and in every work I hope to share my particular understanding and feeling for the subject matter. *Can You Hear the Birds Sing?* (see page 20) and *Everyday is Sunday* (see page 28) are examples of the way that the use of colour can influence the mood of a composition. Both works are part of a series that was inspired by the themes of global warming and climate change, but they evoke different moods: with its cooler, more even-toned colours, *Everyday is Sunday* conveys a calm feeling, whereas in *Can You Hear the Birds Sing?* you can really sense the force and heat of the sun. As there are stronger colours of a higher colour key in this stitched painting, a more vibrant, energetic impression is achieved.

Searching for Klimt (detail)
216 x 150cm (85 x 59in)
The jewel-toned geometric pieces float on a black background, with thick outlines of satin stitch. This work won three awards at the first European Quilt Championships in Holland in 1997.

SURFACE EFFECTS

Most art quilts begin with observation estimating how factors such as pattern, shape and colour values introduce a certain ambience within the subject matter. At the same time, it is very important to notice how colours interrelate and, from this assessment, which colours are likely to be the most significant in revealing the qualities that must be expressed in the quilt. Another thing that can affect my decisions about content and composition is the fact that I never work on one piece in isolation. Usually I am working on a group of works related to a particular series and consequently the pieces inform and influence each other. When I return to a piece I might well bring with me ideas from other works that are in various stages of development.

As I have mentioned, I do not use the conventional methods for dyeing fabrics. This is partly because I seldom confine myself to working in one medium, and partly because I like to keep the colours pure. The range of media I use includes acrylic, Procion MX dye, bleach and collage. The majority of the cloth I use is painted with acrylic, heat fixed after 24 hours. Try using small tubs of Dylon paint – they are very good for painting and printing on fabric. For information on simple surface techniques, see chapter 1, pages 14–21.

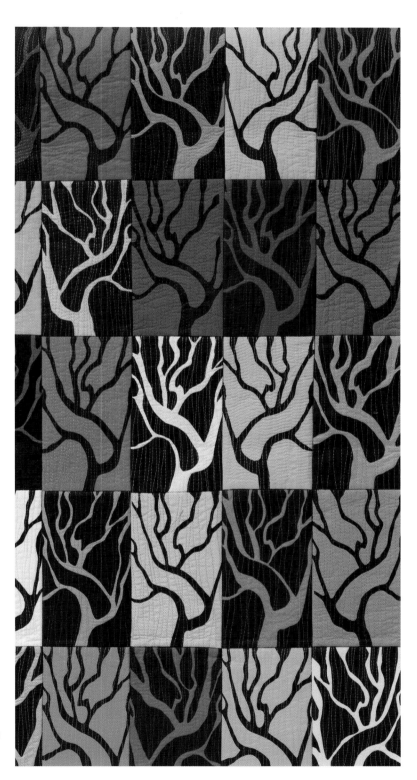

Twigs (detail)
91.5 x 91.5cm (36 x 36in)
Simple black sateen branches create a silhouette against plain-coloured backgrounds, depicting the start of spring growth. Planning the piece in my mind and laying it out in its pieces and sections allows me to see the wholeness and feel the certainty of the composition.

EXERCISE 4: USING SKELETAL SHAPES

In this exercise plain flat colour is used to create an improvised block based on the Daisy collage (shown opposite). This is a crisp, simple contemporary design using four colours. The instructions are to make a basic 45 × 45cm (18 × 18in) block.

Materials and equipment

- 45 × 45cm (18 × 18in) each of plain white cotton, iron-on medium-weight interfacing, wadding (batting) or interlining, and calico (muslin) for the backing
- A few plain colour pre-fused cotton fabrics (keep it simple: I have used white, orange, turquoise and black).
- Sharp scissors or a rotary cutter, mat and acrylic ruler (whichever you prefer working with)
- Iron and ironing board
- Greaseproof (bakery) paper (to protect your iron and board when fusing fabrics)
- Pressing cloth and spray gun
- Sewing machine
- Assorted machine embroidery threads (floss)

Method

1. Prepare your foundation background by ironing the rough side of the interfacing to the wrong side of the plain white cotton square.
2. Free cut your pre-fused fabrics into petal shapes of differing sizes. If you prefer, you can draw the shapes directly onto the paper backing and then cut.
3. Place your background square, right side facing, on an ironing board or working surface. Peel the backing paper off the petals and start to lay them on the background, right side up and rough side down.
4. Layer in a sequence, placing the largest down first, overlapping with the medium and finishing with the smallest. Use your eye to place and layer the shapes and work from the centre to the outer edges. Use your imagination: scatter, overlap, or leave spaces between the petals to allow the background to

show through. Periodically cover with the greaseproof (bakery) paper and hot press to anchor the shapes as you layer.
5. Once you are satisfied with the placement, cover with a cloth, spray and press with a hot iron so that the design is firmly anchored into position.
6. To prepare for stitching, place the calico (muslin) backing right side down, add the layer of wadding (batting) or interlining, then place the collage on top right side up. Pin the layers together.
7. Stitch random grid lines through the three layers, using a straight stitch and a contrasting coloured thread (floss), taking the pins out as you go. Repeat this process until the background is stitched to your satisfaction.
8. Finally, press again and trim any thread ends. The block is now ready to be turned into a cushion, a small hanging or used as part of a larger-scale quilt.

Daisy
Each panel measures 40 x 40cm (16 x 16in)
When you are exploring a particular idea, it is interesting to make a number of works in this way to be developed together as a theme.

5 DESIGN AND CREATIVE PLAY

RESPONDING INSTINCTIVELY

Just as I do not work by traditional methods, similarly there is no standard procedure that I follow when planning new work. The approach that I adopt for a particular piece is determined by the nature of the subject matter and my reaction to it. The formal elements of a subject, such as pattern, shape and colour, are the most striking and I concentrate on these. Inevitably, the finished works have a strong, abstract quality.

The flexibility to interpret subjects according to your personal response is essential; always working to an established, defined method is obviously limiting, both in its intuitive scope and in helping to expand and develop your improvised skills. You may find that the more you work at the process, the less need there is to rely on some form of preliminary drawing.

The pieces *Nike All Alone*, *Spring Field* and *Winter Field* by Danish quilt artist Charlotte Yde (see below, opposite

and page 86) demonstrate her great fondness for fabric and folds – preferably in abundance. Many of the old Greek and Roman statues depict folded textiles in a magnificent way and to her the art of that period represents our roots and the democratic culture in Europe. She is currently working on a series in which she juxtaposes old Greek or Roman statues with contemporary figures.

Nike All Alone
Charlotte Yde
53 x 140cm (21 x 55in)
When Charlotte was young she chose to study Greek and Latin in school and learned to love art from the classical period. This piece depicts a rather rough-stitched, sketch-like representation of Nike, the goddess of Victory.

Deconstructed Spring series – Spring Field and Winter Field
(opposite and over page)
Charlotte Yde
140 x 112cm (55 x 44in)
On her new quilts Charlotte has only used her own dyed or printed fabrics, most of which have been printed using the deconstructed screen printing method. She has combined this with digital embroidery – another of her favourite techniques at the moment. One of the series using these techniques is about the seasons, used as a metaphor for life and time passing.

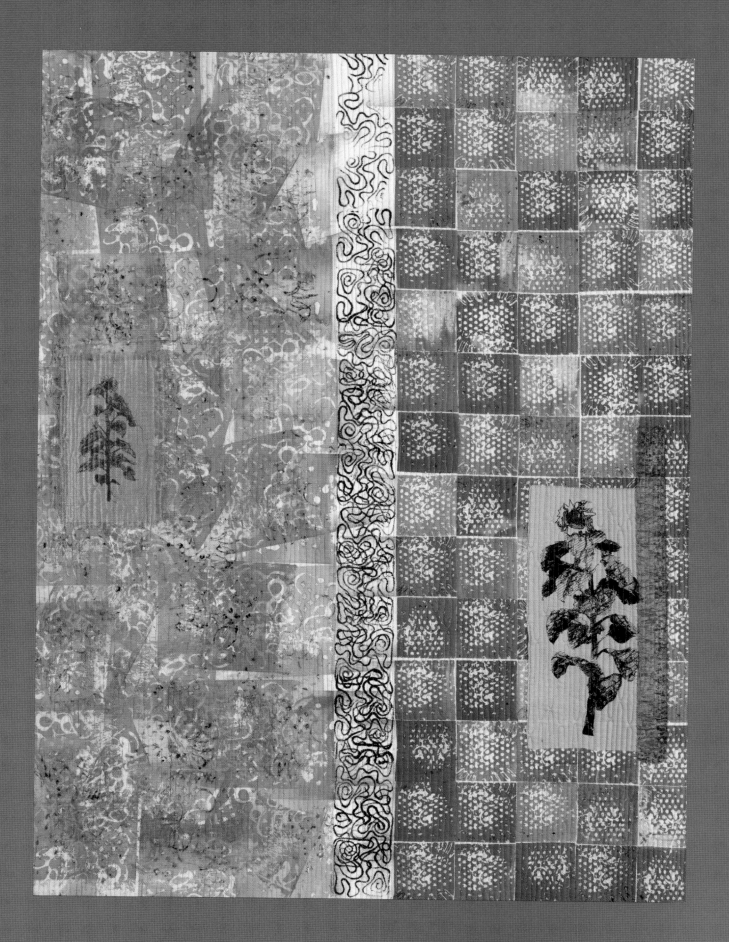

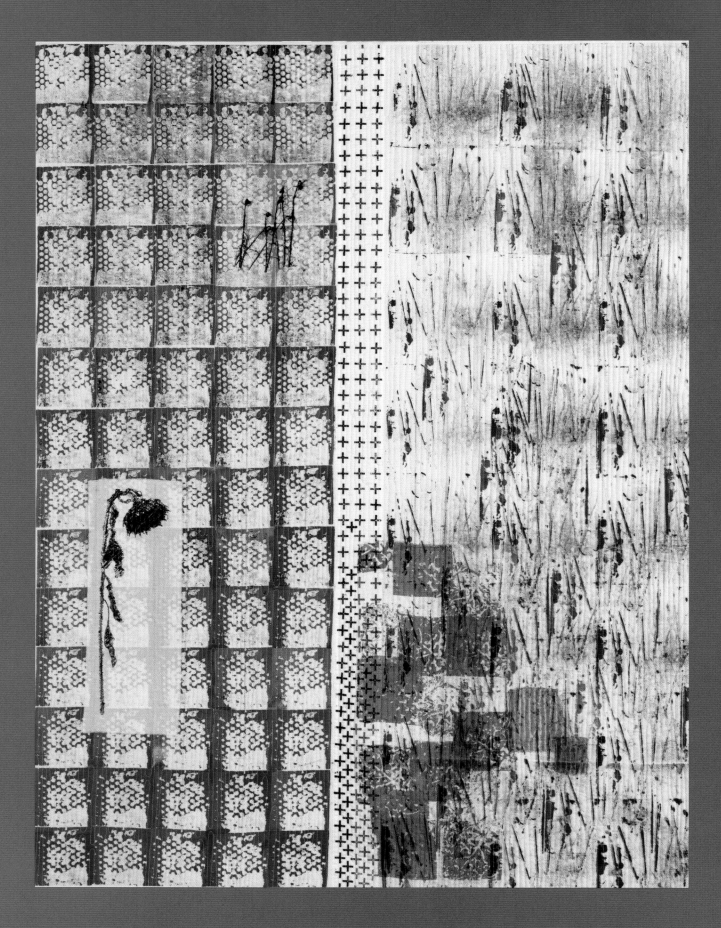

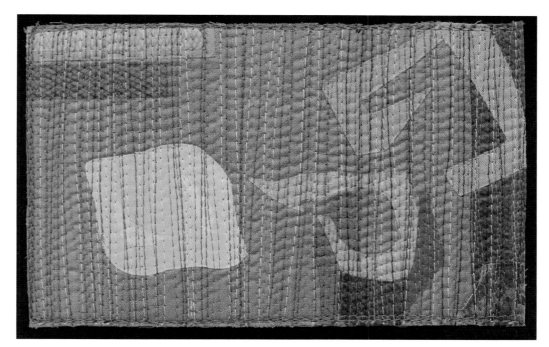

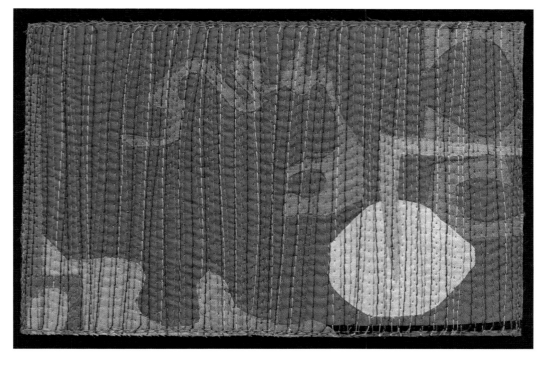

When I look at a subject I mostly see it as colour against colour, and I begin by working with cutting shapes and layering colour rather than by drawing with a pencil, or painting with a brush. I look for the pattern of shapes within the composition and I regard objects and background shapes as equal contributing elements. When this approach is taken to its logical conclusion, with the objects simplified and adjusted to work in a closer pictorial harmony with their surroundings, you can see that an abstract outcome is inevitable. Sometimes not all of my work is completely abstract – there is usually a slight resemblance to the original idea or subject matter. This is evident in the *Orange* and *Bitter Lemon* collages shown above.

PLAY

Perhaps the most important – yet probably the most underrated – element of the process of creating art is that of play. Far from being frivolous, play is the very core of creativity and it is an intensely personal process, since it is often when playing that artists develop ideas and find their own voice. Play is a journey of discovery, the chance to explore ideas, to see what materials can do and what can be created with them. In many ways it's the most exciting part of the creative process.

Good work comes from open-mindedness and intuition – the confidence to rely on personal judgement backed up by experimentation and visual research – rather than doggedly following a preconceived idea. The final piece of work exhibited in a gallery is really only a small part of the artist's labour. One of the biggest mistakes a beginner can make is to concentrate on the final outcome: the pot, the basket, the print. Of course, the final piece must work, but creativity is much more fickle than that. Concentrating on success so often cramps the imagination and results in a rather static and lifeless creation. It is easy to overlook elements that might be worth exploring and might ultimately lead to more exciting work.

Tempting though it is to rush to start, time spent experimenting with materials, making samples, exploring new ways of making, and playing with line and colour will not be wasted but will result in work that is more personal and has more depth than a more direct and superficial approach might yield. Working intuitively rather than constantly referring to drawings is a spontaneous approach that will be more stimulating, allowing the final piece to evolve naturally.

Collecting and selecting objects is also part of creative play. Although this may seem like a digression, for artists who use a variety of materials it is while they are handling such objects that textural qualities are absorbed and vital visual decisions made. I also find inspiration in form and its relationship to cell structures and chemical formulas. While not trying to mimic any scientific methods, many of my processes begin with an attempt to visually interpret a form or the relationship described in it. The quilts *pH 2.0* and *pH 2.2* (see opposite and below), show how mixing specific media because of its distinct properties and characteristics is a key factor in expressing an idea in the most successful way.

pH 2.0 *(right)*
140 x 125cm
(55 x 49¼in)
The background blocks in this piece are made from stitched interfacing with fused silk and cotton collage making up the postcard-sized centres. The inspiration for the quilt came from photographs of cell structures and chemical formulas – *pH 2.0* is the first in a series of three.

pH 2.2 **(detail)** *(left)*
140 x 125cm
(55 x 49¼in)
Inspiration for this work came from photographs of cell structures and chemical formulas. This series is essentially about different ways of describing the patterns in cell structures using layered, free-cut shapes in various mixed medias.

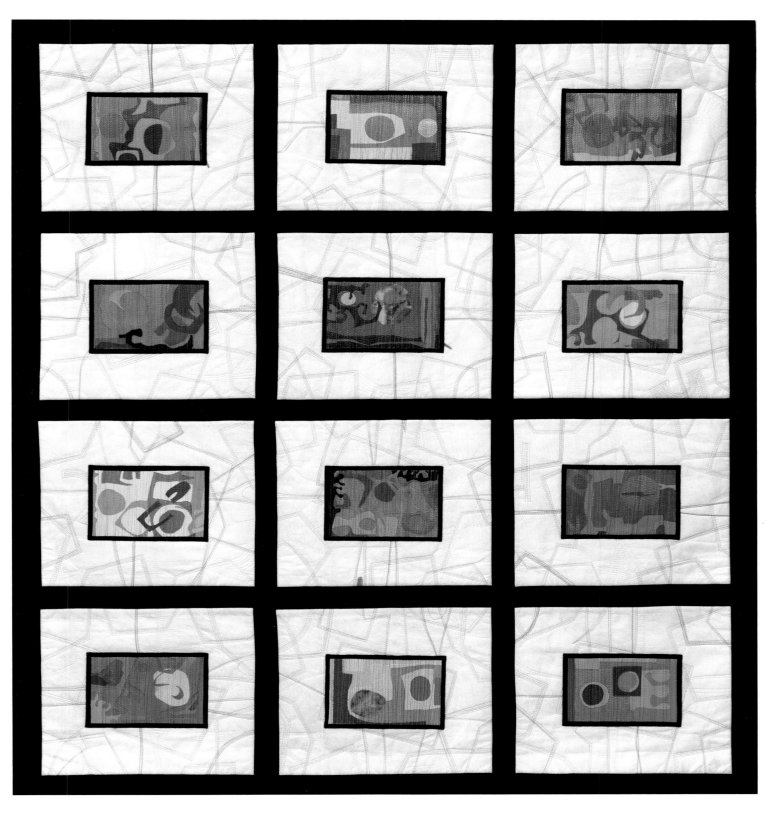

Freedom in restraint

Although play assumes freedom, it does not benefit from lack of direction. It may sound contradictory, but freedom thrives on restraint. Every game has defined rules – their function is not intended to restrict play, but as something to lean on. When using improvisation it is important to give yourself direction in your activity to prevent yourself from just muddling along. The effect of playing with shapes and colour will turn out to be greater if you associate it with limits and restrictions.

Imposing certain limits on a study exercise can steer our creative thinking in a particular direction. This restriction forces us to dig deep in the given direction, which may lead to new discoveries. Without direction, and therefore with a profusion of options, we search more superficially and are more quickly inclined to look for yet more lines of approach. Admittedly this gives a broad outlook, but as far as depth is concerned, it misses the mark. Limits encourage more intensive exploration. Diversity confuses and diffuses our energy. So you can see that direction and limitation will activate your creativity more than superficially wandering about among an overabundance of alternatives.

pH 2.1 (detail)
140 x 130cm (55 x 51in)
This collage was inspired by photographs of cell structures and chemical formulas and is contained in laminated pockets, giving the quilt a semi-translucent appearance

DESIGN ELEMENTS

Quilt art is created with visual features, or elements of design, which work together. Learn to identify these elements in paintings, sculpture and nature, and you will learn more about composition. Creating a composition can vary from being direct and extremely spontaneous to being carefully constructed and well thought out, and it is useful to know which specific aspects to consider:

• What size is the support material: large, small, square, horizontal, vertical or narrow?
• What is the proportion and balance like in the shape structure and the plane division?

• What is our view on the picture we want to present? Is it a panoramic view, with a lot of remaining space and background, or does it fill the picture in close-up with scarcely any remaining space?
• Where do we place the point for attention or focal point?
• What are the main features of the composition, which is the main direction and in what direction are the introductory and any executing lines?
• Where do we place our active parts and where should there be calm?

Ice Cold in Alice (detail)
122 x 142cm (48 x 56in)
The name Alice and the town of Alice Springs in Australia was the inspiration for this quilt. When I imagine Alice Springs I envisage bright primary colours pulsating with heat, whereas the name Alice conjures up cold, clear, pastel colours. The shapes used in the quilt are derived from the traditional log cabin pattern. This is a colour-play interpretation of the combination of both versions of Alice: Alice Springs moves geographically up north to polar regions, hence the title *Ice Cold in Alice*! I love the contrast between cool and hot colours with just a dash of black and white and I have tried to convey that in this work.

DESIGN VALUES

The following design values will help you in quilt design – refer to them as you design your quilts.

Balance

A good composition has a certain suspense and balance which is based on opposites and contrast. Suspense is the feeling that something is happening, that there is a certain amount of action.

Factors such as direction, dynamics, dominance and emphasis play a part in this, and our primary and secondary pictorial elements can provide it.

For practical application, it is definitely useful to pay conscious attention to:

- Focal point
- Active and passive elements
- Plane division
- Foreground and background

A composition with informal balance will appear interesting and almost formally balanced, but not identical on each side of the centre. Trust your eye to know whether something appears balanced, whether it is formal or informal. An example of dynamic balance can be seen in *Down South* (right).

Down South
122 x 91.5cm (48 x 36in)
This art quilt was inspired by our once-weekly trip to Weston-Super-Mare, and is based on roadway markings. This piece gave me the scope to create a powerful composition based on bold shapes in strong colours, broken by roadway markings in white interfacing that rest the eye.

Unity or harmony

When all the elements in a design come together in a pleasing arrangement, you have unity or harmony. This can be achieved in any number of ways – in traditional quilts, repeated blocks create harmony. In *Tree of Life* (shown opposite), the repetition of the pieced lines, paired with the gently curved spheres in a random arrangement, is harmonious.

Line

Line is one of the most important elements in art, since it brings energy. Lines can be thick, thin, zigzag, straight, diagonal, curved, aggressive, subtle or calm. You can see them everywhere and find inspiration in unexpected places. Line gives emphasis to ideas, creates a sense of direction, a pattern, and more. Lines can appear in the piecing and quilting of a quilt and in patterned fabric. Managing the lines in a composition is the foundation of good design. Plain coloured fabric works like paint to make line and shape more visible. Line is lively and vigorous; it activates the mind, not by telling a story but by the feeling on which it is based. Continue to study line and work with new colour assignments.

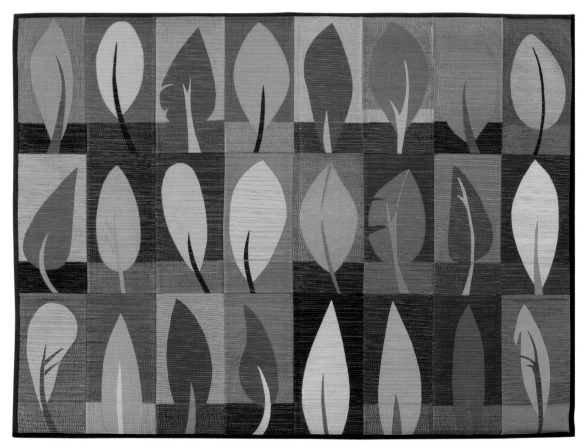

Skeletal Relief *(left)*
61 x 122cm (24 x 48in)
Part of a series made in protest against the massive destruction of the rainforest. My interests lie in how we project our own memories and myths onto woodlands or trees that we may have grown up with; we treasure certain trees and vistas and mourn them when they are destroyed, but continue to have a cold, unfeeling policy towards their management and preservation. This wall quilt illustrates how negative spaces can be created within each block of colour by cutting and applying skeletal shapes of leaves.

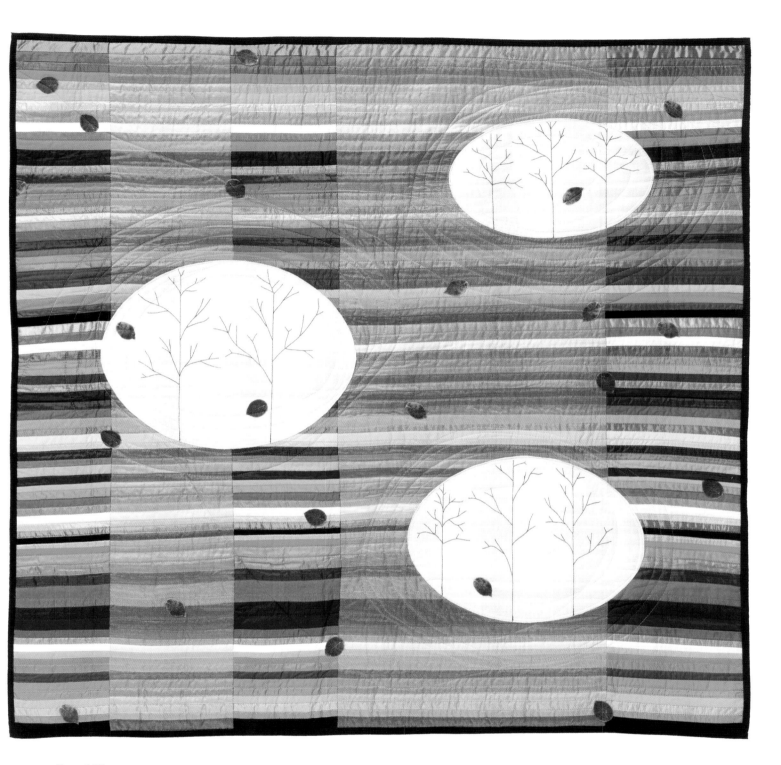

Tree of Life
132 x 127cm (52 x 50in)

This was a follow-on to a quilt I made for the Quilt Art group exhibition on the theme of Moving On. The original quilt was *Black Hole – Mourning Quilt* (see page 69). Nevertheless life carries on regardless no matter how we may be feeling. In *Tree of Life*, hopefulness replaces hopelessness and this is interpreted in the colours, shapes and patterns used in the quilt. Knot-like spheres symbolize the cycles of life and death, summer and winter, dusk and dawn; each new dawn brings a new day and new hope. It is not always simply shape and colour that inspire new ideas; sometimes it is the subject matter itself that is the inspiration.

Scale

The size of a shape in relationship to the size of other shapes in a composition is known as scale. A variety of sizes will make a design more interesting. Larger shapes will feel closer, and smaller ones will feel further away. An area with smaller, detailed shapes can create a centre of interest, inviting the viewer to come closer and take a look. Scale can also refer to the character of shapes and lines in fabric.

Sunflowers
140 x 120cm (55 x 42in)
Every so often I take a break from using strong, bright colours. Even so I still could not resist using a touch of citric yellow and turquoise blue in this piece – the colours go so well with grey…

Shape

Shapes are created when lines are connected and the contrast of negative space around a shape gives it meaning. Pattern is created by repeating shapes.

There are two types of shape:

Geometric shapes: squares, rectangles, triangles and so on.

Organic shapes: rocks, trees, flowers and other natural shapes.

Chrysanthemum
122 x 122cm (48 x 48in)
A partner to *Sunflowers*, made during a break from working with strong, bright colours.

Pattern and texture

Pattern is a repeated decorative design and comes in all shapes and sizes; it can be created with piecing, patterned fabric, quilting designs or stitch. It can point to repetition, shapes, line and texture that appear more or less equally several times, thus forming rhythmical repeats. Pattern accentuates movement and dynamics, but also unity and cohesion. Above all, textures often consist of patterns or rhythmical accents. Short, rhythmical stitching gives an impression of action and various techniques, such as painting, printing and stencilling, are very effective for suggesting rhythm and pattern. Rhythmical movements activate spontaneity and a freer, improvised gesture.

Recognizing and 'seeing' patterns and rhythms in reality is definitely to be recommended – it is possible to draw many quilting ideas and much inspiration from this. Just think of the rhythm of ripples of water, waves, branches or poles. The elements of pattern and rhythm are particularly interesting as the basis for a study exercise – there are artists who fill the entire picture plane with a repetitive pattern, solely on the basis of rhythm.

Applause (detail)
Three panels, each measuring 61 x 99 x 2.5cm (24 x 39 x 1in)
A layered triptych inspired by the primary expression of approval of the act of clapping – or striking the palms of the hands together – in order to create noise. The louder and longer the noise, the stronger the sign of approval.

Texture refers to the effects that disturb or break up the smooth surface of the artwork and it can be organic or more contrived. The varied layers with which we construct our work, everything we apply under, in and over our layer of cloth, provides the surface with variation, unevenness, difference in height or roughness. Texture is therefore an artistic element that greatly defines the picture. It encourages the building up of layers – in this way it gives the impression that the painting has been thoroughly worked through: both literally and figuratively it gives more depth. It gives an inkling of the method and the involvement of the artist. Texture can be achieved through fabric choice, quilting lines, surface design, subtle detail piecing and decorative stitch.

Whichever way you choose, pattern and texture add interest and can be repeated to unite a design. This textural element is demonstrated in the details of the pieces (shown right) by Welsh 'stitch' artist Ruth Harries. Ruth says of her work: 'There are figurative and abstract elements to my work, which represent emotionally charged atmospheres and recollections within the family. I strive to convey emotions triggered by memories. In a response to motherhood, I have delighted in the simple and enviable beauty of a child's confident drawings. I reflect on a house; a place of birth and death and the subtle and intimate traces of life within it, a reflection on the transience of being and our rites of passage. Aspects of my Welsh identity and the use of the Welsh language within my family are also considered. Working directly by letting it grow and develop intuitively and spontaneously, I use machine stitch, achieving subtle variations in colour and tone in a free and expressive way, aiming to express the speed and gesture of a mark. The diverse qualities of mark-making produced by painting, writing and drawing are considered in stitch.'

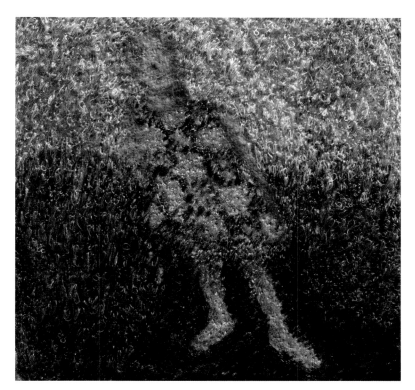

The Path (top) **Ruth Harries**
15 x 15cm (6 x 6in)

Waiting (bottom) **Ruth Harries**
15 x 15cm (6 x 6in)

Shape or plane

Shape is plane are nearly always used with the elements of line and colour. Together they constitute the most obvious art ingredients, which we have understood since childhood. Each has a strongly communicative function, which makes them the most striking visual illustrative language we can have.

The illustrative element of shape or plane is far-reaching:

• It is present in almost every artwork and has a strong compositional function.
• It defines the spatial division of the picture plane and can be either two- or three-dimensional.
• It acts as the subject of a painting and influences the secondary pictorial elements.
• It also has various manifestations and qualities that can be produced in many technical ways.

Abstract shapes

Abstract shapes cannot be named and are free of any function, place, definition and/or format. There are no restrictions from outside, but neither can any outside support be expected. This is precisely the reason why input, intuition, feeling, imagination and creativity are so terribly important here. Abstract shapes can use geometric, symbolic, organic and free shapes, as seen in *Celebration* (see below).

Celebration (detail)
137 x 99cm (54 x 39in)
Inspired by the citrus yellow backing and Japanese prints – the play of light on the yellow suggests an interesting way to divide up the composition and so produce an exciting relationship of shapes and colours.

INTEGRAL ASPECTS

For an art quilt to work successfully, each of its various elements must be of exactly the right strength in relation to the rest. The degree of emphasis given to any one element – whether it is colour, composition, texture or pattern – depends on the subject matter and the intended impact and mood of the work. Essentially, my work evolves rather than develops according to a preconceived plan, and therefore I do not work to a set vision of how the final work will look. However, based on my response to what I observe, I can instinctively make decisions about which features are important in a subject and which materials and techniques are the most appropriate to get me started. Just as any artwork involves a delicate balancing act between its different elements, so does the working process required to produce a successful quilt. While it is vital to know fundamentally what you wish to express in a work, too fixed a notion leaves little room for imagination and spontaneity.

Broken Pot
91.5 x 122cm (36 x 48in)
The background of this piece is made from hand-dyed fabrics inspired by Art Deco pottery, and the design was layered, stitched, cut, rearranged and appliquéd in position. I usually start with an object that has attracted my attention, then I find colours that will complement it in some way, aiming to create an interesting arrangement of colour, shape and form.

Effective combinations

Sometimes I use household objects for inspiration; these can include colourful pots, vases and dishes, textiles and so on. The way that these objects are perceived is largely an intuitive process – start with one object that has attracted your attention, and then add others that contrast or complement it in some way to build a sound composition with interesting relationships of shape, colour and texture. Try to prevent the composition from looking too contrived, and do not necessarily stick to the initial arrangement. When layering your shapes, remove an object or change the position of something if you think the composition will benefit. A single group might initially be the basis for more than one quilt. Another point worth bearing in mind is that a simple design, such as in *Little Brown Jug* 1 and 2 (see right), is often more effective than a complex arrangement. The objects are essentially a starting point: after a while they become less important as you become more involved with the colour relationships and surface qualities.

Little Brown Jug 1
(above right)
50 x 30cm (20 x 12in)
Once you begin to think in terms of light, colour and shape, it is surprising how much potential you notice in quite ordinary objects, especially if they are significant in some way, as was the case with these jugs.

Little Brown Jug 2 *(right)*
50 x 30cm (20 x 12in)

My advice is to choose colours and materials that will give both interest and coherence to a quilt, at the same time taking into account the overall mood and impact that you have in mind.

It is wise not to complicate the process too much, so you should keep to a limited number of materials and techniques. Often the most effective approach is to start with a plain fabric (or texture) and subsequently layer over with basic shapes and colours; definition and texture can be further enhanced with more layering and stitch. Having assessed the subject matter, look for colours that are compatible and that will bring out the mood and impact you have in mind. As an example see *Mamgu Gardd* (opposite).

Oasis (detail)
203 x 203cm (80 x 80in)
This was made when my son was constantly playing 'jungle' music and its heavy beat affected my state of mind when working, resulting in a cacophony of shape and colour. The title refers to my search for quiet during this mayhem.

DEVELOPING SKILLS

When you work with improvisation, there is no better way to develop your skills than through trial and error. It is a matter of having the courage, in every composition, to try something new and to work without fear of making mistakes. Results are invariably more effective and ideas tend to evolve with far greater energy and impact when the quilt-making process is positive and uninhibited. The ability to work with confidence and skill relies on experience, and this in turn comes from a willingness to experiment and learn from all the consequent successes and failures.

Mamgu Gardd (detail)
91.5 x 91.5cm (36 x 36in)
By choosing a simple flower shape and being adventurous with colour, you can create some joyful results, such as this quilt, which is full of happy memories.

IMPROVISING WITH MIXED MEDIA

The advantage of using mixed media is that it broadens the range of technical and interpretative possibilities, and additionally it helps to keep work fresh and forward-looking. However, much depends on the individual artist; while I am excited by the mixed-media approach, I accept that other quilt artists are more comfortable with using a single medium.

By mixing your materials and using improvisation, your work will become bolder, with stronger colour emphasis. Your choice of materials will reflect this – I use a lot of flat colour but also enjoy playing with resist and discharge dyeing. It is interesting to note the phases when certain media attract a lot of my attention

and in turn influence the style of my work for a particular one-off or series.

The works by American artist Shelley Brenner Baird (above and opposite) illustrate her use of non-literal narratives on fabric. The marks she uses may be balanced or reckless, austere or angry, surgical or ragged, literal or obscure. In her work images are superimposed on cloth by screen printing, painting and drawing with dyes, paint and bleaching agents, processes both directed and serendipitous, as the reaction with the fabric is instantaneous and slightly out of her control. The exact result is revealed only when the dye residue is washed from the fabric, much like watching a photograph develop in the darkroom.

Nonconforming Parts
Shelley Brenner Baird
81 x 107cm (32 x 42in)
This piece is the result of selection and editing, applying, resisting and removing colour; in other words, fitful starts and stops of creation and destruction. I am inspired by the visual serendipity of the process, the magic of knowing when to stop.

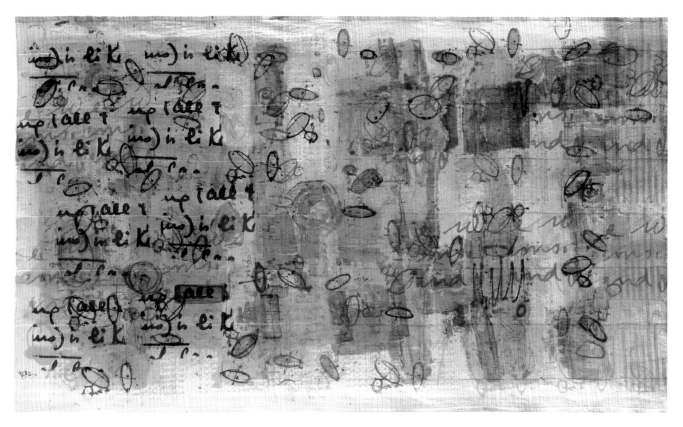

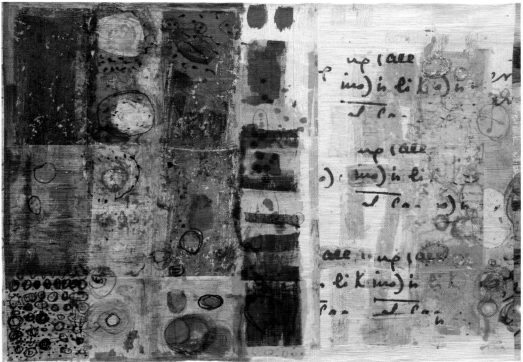

Language and Thought
(above)
Shelley Brenner Baird
112 x 178cm (44 x 70in)
Inspired by the mysterious connection between language and thought, this is a non-literal narrative, a story about time and place told in gestures and layers. Screen printing leaves the surface transfigured by its inherent repetition and immediacy.

Plot *(left)*
Shelley Brenner Baird
107 x 152cm (42 x 60in)
Words and symbols, sequencing and storytelling inspire my work. Unlike a literal narrative, it is about what is imagined rather than evident.

Exploring different media

There is a lot to discover about the way different materials respond and interrelate when used in a mixed-media context. Not only is it essential to get to know the strengths and limitations of each individual material, but also the way it behaves and the range of effects that are possible when it is applied over or beneath a contrasting fabric. It is very easy to make mistakes by being a little too enthusiastic with the use of a particular fabric, or by assuming that if something goes wrong it can instantly be corrected by layering over it. The way forward is to learn from such mistakes, because they should add to your knowledge and experience of a certain fabric or technique.

The main object is to persevere with your collage and accept that mistakes come with the territory, especially if you are true to your feelings and aspirations and are not afraid to test your abilities to the limit. So, in developing skills, it is vital to gain a breadth of understanding of different materials through experimentation and practice. This can be achieved as much through exploratory exercises on scraps of paper as it can by being ambitious within the actual collage process itself.

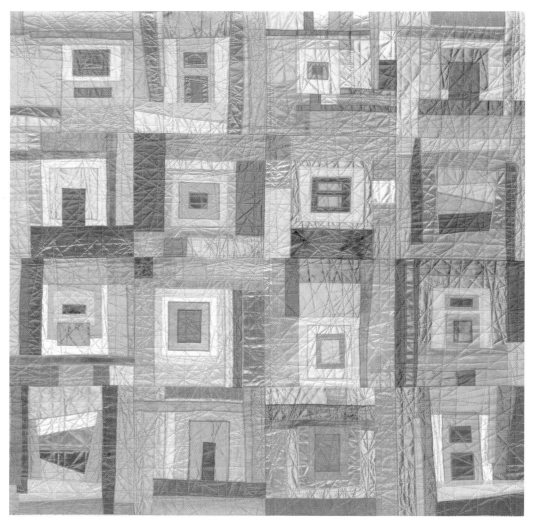

Messages to a Sun God
(right)
150 x 124cm (59 x 49in)
This quilt is a follow on to *Moving Being – Square Dance* (see page 118), and was inspired by the glorious discharge-dyed golden yellow fabric, which originally came from 1930s viscose bedspreads. The cotton used was resist dyed. The quilt represents and symbolizes messages to another being and another place in time.

Interlude
124 x 140cm (49 x 55in)
Every so often I have a break from working with strong, vibrant colours. The fabrics used in this quilt come from 1930s satin viscose bedspreads, and to create soft muted colours I have over-dyed it, using resist and discharge techniques with Procion MX dye and household bleach. This piece is my 'interlude' from using vibrant colours and represents a pause in time.

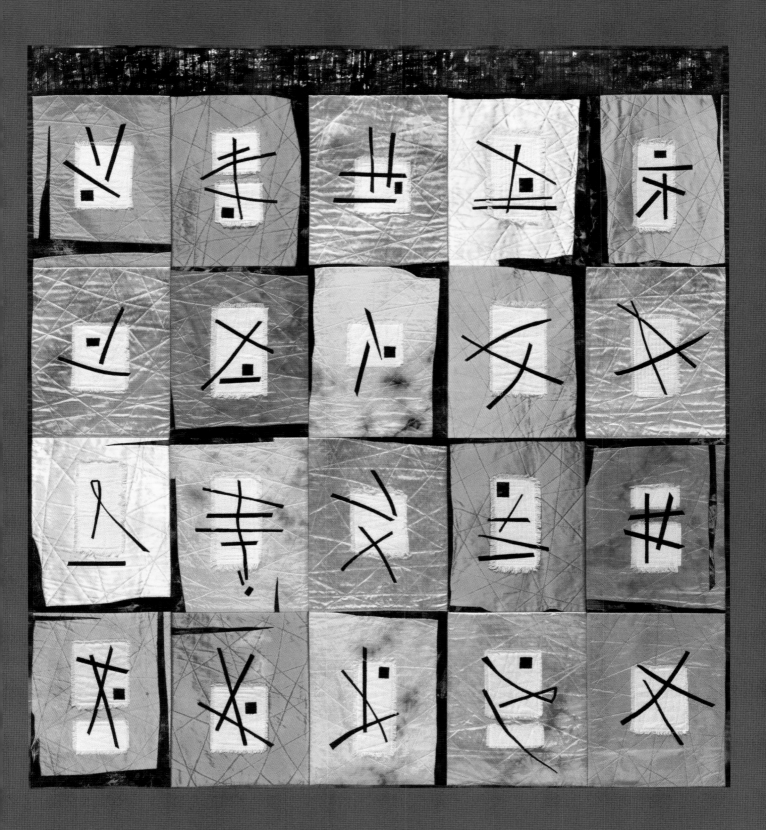

EXERCISE 5: USING A POEM, TEXT OR WORDS AS IMAGERY

This exercise uses text printed across the quilt surface to create an improvised panel based on the *Universal Colours* quilt opposite. These instructions are to make a finished block approximately 30 × 40cm (12 × 16in).

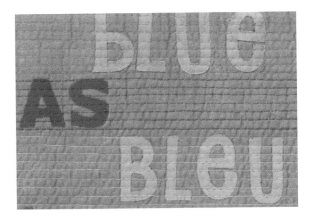

Materials and equipment

- A text poem, verse, or wording that inspires you
- Six 30 × 40cm (12 × 16in) each of coloured cotton fabric, iron-on medium-weight interfacing (for stabilisation), wadding (batting) or interlining and calico (muslin) for backing
- Sharp scissors or a rotary cutter, mat and acrylic ruler (whichever you prefer working with)
- Iron and ironing board
- Greaseproof (bakery) paper to protect your iron and board when fusing fabrics
- Pressing cloth and spray gun
- Computer and printer
- Iron-on transfer paper
- Sewing machine
- Assorted machine embroidery threads (floss)

Method

1. Pick six words for colour – such as blue, green, turquoise – and translate into four different languages.
2. Type the words out on your computer, enlarge, reverse and print out on to iron-on transfer paper.
3. To make the pieced background, select six of the webbing-backed fabrics in matching colours to your chosen words.
4. To prepare the background, cut the cotton fabric and interfacing into six 30 × 40cm (12 × 16in) blocks. Iron the rough side of the interfacing to the wrong side of one of the blocks, using a dry hot iron. Repeat this process on the remaining five blocks.
5. Cut out your printed words and sort into independent colour piles.
6. Take one of the fabric blocks and place it face up on a flat surface. Start applying the matching colour words by laying each face down onto the surface of the corresponding block, and heat transfer following the manufacturer's instructions.
7. When all the words have been applied to all the blocks, lay the blocks out on a flat surface in a sequence of two across by three down. Join the strips using a sewing machine, with a straight stitch and a 1cm (½in) seam allowance.
8. Once you have finished joining all the blocks, open the seams, cover with a cloth, spray and press with a hot iron so that the seam allowances lay flat.
9. To prepare for quilting, place the calico (muslin) backing right side down, add the layer of wadding (batting) or interlining, then place the colour block panel on top, right side up. Pin the layers together.
10. Stitch randomly through the layers many times, using straight stitch and a variety of coloured threads, removing the pins as you go. Repeat until the background is stitched to your satisfaction, and any raw edges are covered.
11. Finally, press, trim, hand-bind the edges and sew a sleeve for hanging on the back near the top edge.

Universal Colours
One of two panels, each measuring 91.5 x 84cm (36 x 33in)
One idea often leads naturally on to another related subject, perhaps using some of the same elements and an identical palette of colours.

6 DISREGARDING THE RULES...

STYLE AND INNOVATION

Quite often particular materials and techniques that you have used, together with the way that you have resolved a certain problem, will inspire other ideas and approaches that are worth pursuing. We now know about the symbolic elements of composition, technique and materials, and so we have arrived at the most essential component of improvisation – the idea, the subject, the theme. If we have no theme, then there is nothing to make.

With originality and involvement in mind, it is very important that you arrive at your own ideas and study tasks independently. You really do not need anyone to get you started. On the basis of your own creativity you are capable of finding your own inspiration and subject matter. Finding your own ideas is at least as important as developing technical skills so make your own reference work containing ideas, subjects, exercises and themes. There is a huge number of sources from which you can draw; the most important thing is to know where to go to look for ideas. As soon as you can introduce some kind of system into this you will be off – just linking the described abstract elements to your knowledge of materials, technique, composition and construction gives you a huge arsenal of possibilities.

American quilt artist Ginny Smith is no stranger to diversity. She says of her work: 'Quilting is the perfect medium for me. Every step is enjoyable, from the beginning concept to the final stitches. To me, quilts are poems: poems to colour and fabric; poems to history and meaning. I draw inspiration from many diverse sources and from quilts: old, odd, energetic quilts with uncomfortable colour combinations and eccentric stitching to historical textiles: holy relics, quilted armour and story-telling embroideries. Contemporary artists are important influences, such as Elizabeth Murray, Anselm Kiefer, Frank Stella, and I often revisit old favourites like Joseph Cornell and Henri Rousseau. I especially enjoy folk and so-called outsider art and lately the pencil drawings of Martin Ramirez. Finally I draw upon the natural world and the myths, legends and folktales we have devised to explain that world. I especially like to make use of birds, appointing them the representatives of the natural world. Lately my quilts have all contained birds, in various states of reaction to troubling times.'

Anxiety Won (right)
Ginny Smith
175 x 159cm
(68¾ x 62½in)
This is both a reference to current anxious times and to old quilts, which sometimes featured an urn with flowers (here bare sticks) and birds. The words are the artist's own.

Maybe the Test of Migration (left)
Ginny Smith
174 x 138cm
(68½ x 54¼in)
In this quilt the birds are missing, leaving only the flowers, and asking the question, 'Where are the birds?'.

FRESH CHALLENGES

One of the main joys of working with improvisation is that it can give free rein to your creativity – in fact the message is: disregard the rules. Even if you are a complete novice you can discover how to make exciting designs using a medley of different colours, fabrics, threads and stitch. Ignore all the limitations that may have been freely passed on by too-conservative teachers, family, friends and relations. Savour all the enthusiasm and suggestions that you can gather from those around you. Try out, explore and experiment with ideas and materials, and attempt to translate both into unorthodox forms. New technology and fibres are constantly being created and apart from being just functional, most hold very exciting possibilities for creative exploration.

Dee Jay Installation
**Each panel 30 x 30cm
(12 x 12in)**
Inspired by my son's love of mixing music combined with a traditional patchwork technique.

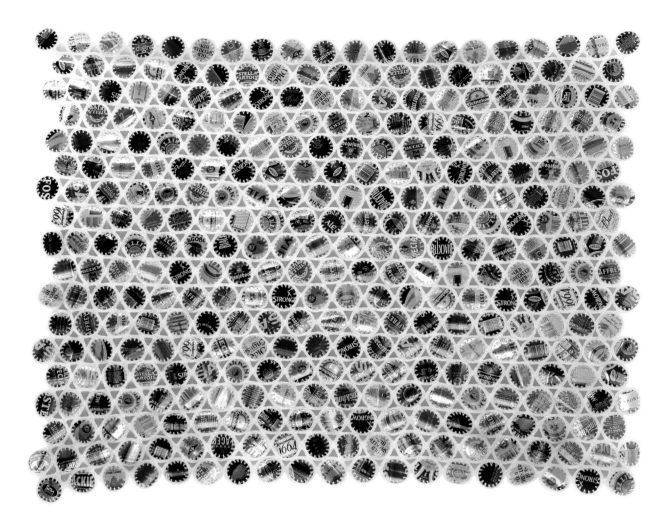

There are basically two types of quilt artists. One group will enjoy working through a number of exercises and experimentation to gain greatest satisfaction from the creative potential of familiar and unusual materials, allied to unorthodox means of reaching desired results. The second group will be hesitant to experiment, yet produce exciting work with traditional techniques as features. Whichever group you fall into you will no doubt face the question of whether the work is complete or not. From this point of view a richly worked textile piece is visually more exciting than one that is not.

The success of working spontaneously depends very largely on how important a role creativity plays in it. This involves questioning or even disregarding various rules held dear by the purists and the traditional quilt-maker. The fascination of creative work lies in using your intuition when exploring new possibilities and finding innovative solutions to problems – there are no limits to the ways and means in which you can translate colours, fabric and textures into unique pieces of art. There is always something new to discover.

Keeping the Homeless Warm
183 x 183cm (72 x 72in)
In this version of a crocheted Welsh blanket, the pieces represent studies in contrasts: softness versus rigidity; minimal form versus maximum pattern; handcrafted appearance versus machine aesthetic. The material content also brings to light many of the uncomfortable truths of our contemporary society.

Part of the pleasure of working with textiles, and quilt art in particular, is its wide potential for being manipulated to create a new textured surface. The English fibre artist Sandie Welch describes her work as follows: 'My aims are to develop and promote my particular art form. To challenge and cross the perceived boundaries between craft and fine art. For as long as I can remember I have been fascinated by the texture, make-up and construction of all materials and fabrics, whether natural or man-made. My earliest influences in fabrics were from antique Welsh quilts. I studied their construction and spent several years restoring decayed and damaged quilts and fabrics; the element of texture has always been of vital importance to me. I use a variety of techniques in my artwork; these include collage, wire and thread, weaving, layering, sculpting and manipulation to create new textured fabrics. I also enjoy using a diverse range of collected and recycled materials in order to make my three-dimensional constructions.'

Toffee Bag Wall Quilt
Sandie Welch
183 x 183cm (72 x 72in)
Each Suffolk Puff (yo-yo) in this quilt is an individual mixed-media collage drawn together with thread. The piece is inspired mostly by the artist's love of colour and texture.

Tea with Mrs Jones
Sandie Welch
50cm x 30cm (12 x 20in)
Inspired by the taking of tea with Mrs Jones, listening to tales of days gone by and then her giving me boxes of lace and beautiful dress fragments to use in my artwork.

Release 1 (right)
Helen Foroughi
40 x 30 x 20cm (16 x 12 x 8in)
The pieces are not pre-designed as such, but rather evolve from a basic idea the same way as one would work on a painting, the qualities of the materials playing a large part in the decision-making process.

Divine Lote Tree (far right)
Helen Foroughi
56cm x 20cm x 20cm (22 x 8 x 8in)
You can develop the scope and success of your work by introducing new ideas, new materials and techniques. Also, in a mixed-media context, the extent to which one medium is used in relation to another can obviously have a dramatic influence on the visual and emotional impact of your finished compositions.

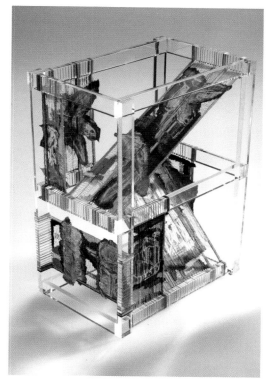

A sense of design may be inspired by the mere sight of a group of coloured threads placed against one or more coloured fabrics. The colour relationships may express a mood, or an emotion, which can be emphasized by the techniques applied. Every fine or applied artist has his or her own method of creating an image or achieving an object from the first rough sketch to the final moment of completion.

The recent work of English fibre artist Helen Foroughi (above and right) pushes the boundaries of traditional tapestry and challenges conventional weaving by exploring an individual and unique approach, weaving on Perspex frames and 3D forms. Working with a combination of handmade paper, linen, silk, cotton, metallic yarns and nylon monofilament, she incorporates lino-printed images in her pieces. In some areas transparent or coloured monofilament is woven loosely between the warps, giving a filigree effect, or the weft is forced between tightly packed warps to create a textured surface, while in other areas conventional tapestry techniques are used.

Toran Screen
Helen Foroughi
40 x 48.5 x 19cm (16 x 19¼ x 7½in)
Helen's work develops from a process of working instinctively with the materials, building up and incorporating the printed images into the weave structure.

Moving Being – Square Dance
122 x 122cm (48 x 48in)
I am interested in the interplay of shape and form and how randomly pieced shapes and use of colour build into recognizable forms to create a perception of the idea in the viewer's mind. The pieced figures are simple but varied, uncertain and random, which creates a kind of visual rhythm. Detail of layering shown below.

The concept of desire is a central part of my newest work – the consumption of material goods, the need we have to buy everything at least once, the lure of luxury and extravagance, food fantasies and issues of control are all given a voice. For the *Mad World* series (see opposite) and *Bed of Roses* collage (see page 122), I have recycled plastic carrier bags and woven them into tubular constructions. These materials are not as precious as gold or silver but in many ways reflect more accurately the values of today's throw-away society.

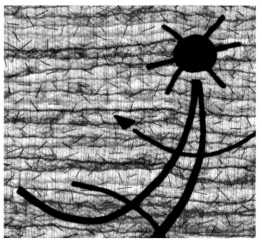

THEMES AND VARIATIONS

No two artists will interpret the same subject in an identical manner. Moreover, there are many variations in the way that any subject can be interpreted, irrespective of individual style. For instance, you can create an entirely different result by using other media, colour combinations or working processes; by trying different scale and format ideas; or by accentuating alternative qualities and aspects of the subject. Another possibility is to show the same subject from different viewpoints.

It is interesting to make a number of works in this way, based on a particular theme. Often, one approach develops naturally into another, because during the working process – having made a certain decision – I am aware that there are other possibilities that will lead the piece towards a different conclusion.

Mad World –
Tree Warmer
173 x 33cm (68 x 13in)
This woven plastic bag construction was inspired by the 21st century craze for consumer consumption and the prohibitive waste it creates – also the great need we have to protect our trees.

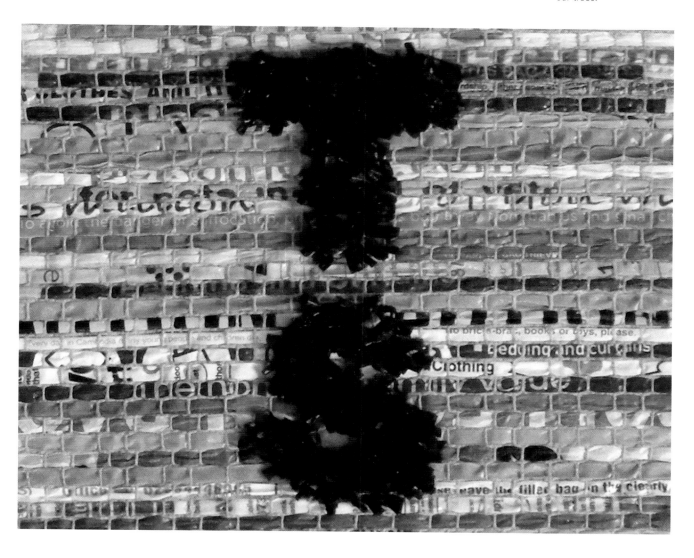

NEW MEDIA AND TECHNOLOGY

Textiles are an excellent medium for the expression of identity and transmission of new ideas. When you attach imagery to the surface of cloth it can instantly give the image new meaning; we begin to associate with the image and might see it as having a spiritual significance or purpose, or an expressive or symbolic ability. Pieces can be made by merging computer image manipulation, digital printing, textile dyeing and finishing with construction. In applying digital textile printing technology we set aside traditional quilt-making concepts, allowing new models to develop. As they do so, the relationships between form, function and creative expression will also develop. The sources of reference and inspiration that provide stimulation offer endless scope for the development of new and exciting work. As an example see *Kaleidoscope*, from the *Digitally Distressed* series (see below), which came from a scanned piece of collage (*Colour Block* – see page 42), that I have manipulated in Photoshop and transfer-printed onto cloth.

Digitally Distressed –
Kaleidoscope *(below)*
New Wave *(right)*
Each block measures
61 x 61cm (24 x 24in)
Kaleidoscope and *New Wave* are two related images that represent further examples of digital experimentation, which lends itself to an abstract or semi-abstract interpretation.

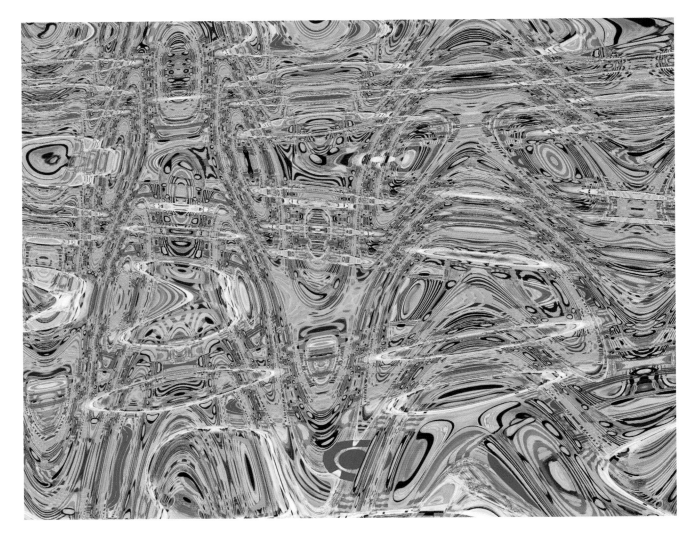

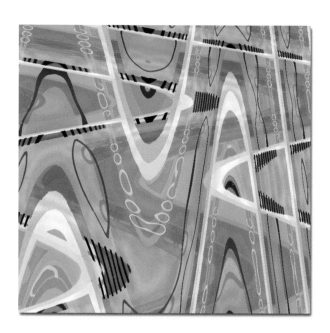
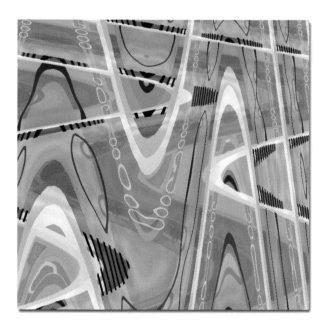
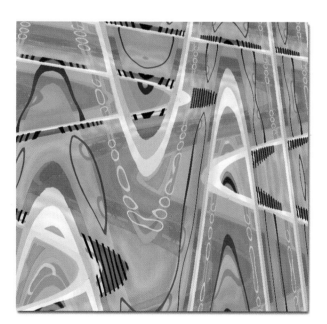

IMPROVISED ABSTRACTION

I think of improvisation and abstraction as an exploration of the rich visual properties of colour and line that define, energize and animate the quilt surface. Abstraction relies on shapes and marks that show no obvious link with the subject matter. It is arrived at in consideration of various aspects of colour theory; or derived from an extensive process of analysis and simplification, initially from looking at objects that are no longer identifiable; or works are expressed completely intuitively, perhaps inspired by a piece of music or in response to some inner passionate feeling about something. One idea is to focus on a section of a work that you have already finished and then enlarge this area as the basic composition for an entirely new work. Or use your computer to scan in previous developed sample material and manipulate pieces from that.

Bed of Roses (detail)
101.5 x 61cm (40 x 24in)
Inspired by the sayings and the trials and tribulations experienced in organizing an exhibition having been given only six weeks' notice!

DESIGN IMPACT

To explore other types of reference and begin new skills with different media and techniques can be extremely instructive and inspirational, but what ultimately counts is how effective your work is in communicating your feelings and ideas. In every composition, design and colour are the elements to think about most, because if either of these is weak the full impact of the work will be lost. Therefore, when introducing a new approach, always consider it in relation to the composition and colour values.

The *Fecund Thoughts* series of works (shown right), by English textile artist Alison Mercer, penetrate the real and the imaginary. Alison says of her work, 'When I am making I am absorbed in the activity, working intuitively and guided by the thoughts and revelations that crafting uncovers. I want to discover who I am and why stitch is so important to me. Each object becomes a revelation and a token of memory. The stitched objects, books and documentation reflect my compulsion to express the relationship between the self and the outside world. Every object I make affirms continuity for future generations and adds an esoteric mystery to a world that has paved over some of its ancient magic. I hope an audience will view the archive with curiosity recognizing the need to revisit the past and make connection for themselves.'

Fecund Thoughts (Pink Boobies) *(right)*
Alison Mercer
44 x 68.5cm (17 x 27in)
The stitched garments and objects Alison creates explore the issues of stitching and unstitching self-identity using everyday activity. *Fecund Thoughts* is a series of visuals that embrace this practice and aim to bring together the varied visual documentation collected in connection to her ancestors. She utilizes memory, historical imagery, personal reflection and myths of her female ancestors, creating intuitively crafted, tangible fabric surfaces imbued with layered personification.

Fecund Thoughts *(above)*
Alison Mercer
35.5 x 40cm (14 x 16in)
During a recent Arts Council residency at the Ysbyty Gwynedd hospital in 2008–2011 Alison based herself within the maternity and labour wards, collecting research to transfer to her fibre art surfaces. The *Fecund Thoughts* series embodies the results of this research, quilting and re-structuring the surfaces of fabric, creating fleshy, maternal surfaces.

EXERCISE 5: USING SHAPE AND STITCH

This exercise uses plain fabric to create an improvised block based on the *Black Blob* photograph shown opposite. These instructions are to make a basic 30 × 40cm (12 × 16in) block.

Materials and equipment

- 30 × 40cm (12 × 16in) each of plain yellow cotton fabric, iron-on medium-weight interfacing, wadding (batting) or interlining, and calico (muslin) for the backing
- Two plain colour cotton fabrics, pre-backed with fusible webbing. For this piece I am using black and red
- Sharp scissors or a rotary cutter, mat and acrylic ruler (whichever you prefer working with)
- Iron and ironing board
- Greaseproof (bakery) paper to protect your iron and board when fusing fabrics
- Pressing cloth and spray gun
- Embroidery hoop
- Sewing machine
- Assorted machine embroidery threads (floss)

Method

1. Prepare your foundation background by ironing the rough side of the interfacing to the wrong side of the plain yellow fabric square.
2. Cut one piece of the webbing-backed fabric (here I've used the red) into matching long and short lengths and cut a small egg shape out of the other colour.
3. Place your yellow background square right side upward on an ironing board or working surface. Peel the backing papers off the fabric strips and begin layering them in a sequence on the background. Use your eye, placing the strips right side up, rough side down, and working 1cm (½in) in from the outer edges.
4. Periodically cover the work with the greaseproof (bakery) paper and hot press to anchor the shapes as you layer.
5. Peel the paper off the egg-shaped piece and position it in centre of the block, right side up and rough side down. Cover with greaseproof (bakery) paper and lightly press.

6. Once you are satisfied with the placement, cover with a cloth, spray and press with a hot iron so that the design is firmly anchored into position.
7. Secure the block in the hoop, drop the feed dogs on your machine and using black thread, stitch in a random motion around the centre shape.
8. To prepare for quilting, place the calico (muslin) backing right side down, add the layer of wadding (batting) or interlining, then place the colour block panel on top right side up. Pin the layers together.
9. Using transparent monofilament thread and a straight stitch, randomly stitch through the three layers a multitude of times, taking the pins out as you go and making sure to cover any raw edges. Repeat this process until the background is stitched to your satisfaction.
10. Finally, press again and trim any thread ends. The block is now ready to be turned into a cushion, a small hanging or used as part of a larger-scale quilt.

Black Blob
Each panel 30 x 40cm (12 x 16in)
When you are exploring a particular idea, it is interesting to make a number of works in this way to be developed together as a theme.

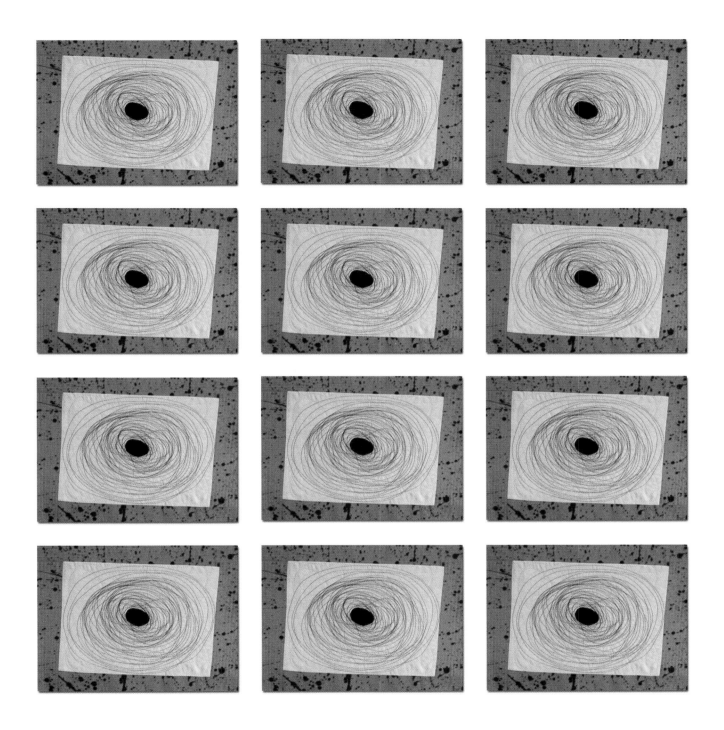

Silk Geometric
91.5 x 112cm (36 x 44in)
Richly patterned shapes in vibrantly coloured silk fabrics.
Raw-edge appliqué and dense machine stitching are used
to create this one-of-a-kind work.

I hope that by now I have made you enthusiastic about the idea of using your intuition to make art as a valuable, ongoing part of your creative life. Now that you have been introduced to the abstract method of improvisation and its tools, you can go on and discover and try new themes, source elements, surface design, different materials and new techniques on which to build. Once you have gained your confidence with colour, do not be afraid to use it to express your ideas in a personal way.

Here are a few more tips to help you on your way:
• Do the exercises that I have given you throughout this book to get you started on new ideas and keep going forward with your artwork.
• Use your sketchbook and portfolios to build up your reserve of ideas for future work; this will help sustain your interest in making art and art quilts.

• Attend art classes and art exhibitions to get inspired – but suppress any tendency to copy the works that you have seen.
• Take photographs or make sketches of the things that you see around you and try to view your environment in different ways. Learn to see 'abstractly' and discover rhythms, contrasts in colour, shapes, compositions, and so on, which one by one can be an excuse to go and paint.
• Be open to new ideas. Cultivate a healthy curiosity and desire to experiment and experience the pleasure that free and spontaneous improvisation can give you.
• Don't become lazy and let your creative life slip away just because you feel blocked. Instead, work through these phases. Aim for creativity, expression, originality and individuality and be led by your own talent.
•Always make art for yourself. No one ever knows what type of art will sell or be popular, so set aside these notions, and allow yourself to create your art freely.

IN CONCLUSION

Above all, what I hope I have managed to convey in this book is that, while techniques and subject matter are important, ultimately the factor that most determines satisfaction and success from quilt-making is the ability to express ideas in a personal way. While I am not a believer in traditional methods, which I think tend to stifle the emotional content and impact of the work, I still respect the process. Quilt-making is never simply a matter of process or skill. It is the artist's interpretation of something seen and experienced, or the originality and

imagination shown in expressing an idea, that makes all the difference between producing a straightforward image of what is there and creating a work that is evocative, challenging, interesting and exciting.

Whether your work has a representative or abstract bias is up to you – whichever approach you adopt, I hope it brings you as much pleasure and reward as I continue to enjoy from my quilt-making. As I've said from the beginning of this book: 'Use your intuition and let it guide you.' And, 'Don't think – do!'

INDEX

CREDITS/ARTIST CONTACTS

All photographs by Jonathan James at Pinegate Photographics (www.pinegate.co.uk) except the following exceptions: pages 12, 18, 19, 21, 23, 25, 31, 39, 40, 44, 45, 50, 54, 55, 68, 70 (top), 71, 80, 82, 83, 101, 102, 105, 114, 119, 120, 121, 122, 124, 125 Bethan Ash; 22 Jim Corbin; 34 Jayne Willoughby-Scott; 36, 37 Maryline Collioud-Robert; 48 Marianne Häni; 52, 53 Lisa Call; 56, 57 Tom Dimond; 106, 107 Shelley Brenner Baird; 112, 113 Steve Tuttle.

Bethan Ash: www.bethanash.co.uk
Shelley Brenner Baird: www.shelleybrennerbaird.com
Elizabeth Brimelow: www.quiltart.eu
Lisa Call: www.lisacall.com
Maryline Collioud-Robert: www.marylinecollioudrobert.com
Cynthia Corbin: www.cynthiacorbin.com
Helen Foroughi: www.helenforoughi.co.uk
Marianne Häni: www.mariannehaeni.com

Ruth Harries: www.ruthharries.co.uk
Terry Jarrard-Dimond: www.terryjarrarddimond.com
Alison Mercer: www.alisonmercer.com
Alison Moger: www.mogerdesigns.com
Ginny Smith: www.ginnysmithart.com
Janet Twinn: www.janettwinn.co.uk
Sandie Welch: www.sandiewelch.co.uk
Jane Willoughby-Scott: www.jaynewilloughbyscott.com

Bethan Ash is a professional quiltmaker and teacher with a background in fashion design. She has exhibited widely and her work has been bought by museums in the UK and US, including the Museum of Arts and Design in New York. She is a member of the prestigious international Quilt Art group.

Also available:

Colour in Art Quilts
Janet Twinn
9781849940009

Connecting Art to Stitch
Sandra Meech
9781906388102

Landscape in Contemporary Quilts
Ineke Berlyn
9780713489743

To receive regular email updates on forthcoming Anova titles, email update@anovabooks with your area of interest in the subject field.

Visit www.anovabooks.com for a full list of our available titles.